Pilgrim in the Parish

A SPIRITUALITY FOR LAY MINISTERS

by

Virginia Sullivan Finn

paulist press ♦ new york ♦ mahwah

Library of Congress
Catalog Card Number: 85-61742

ISBN: 0-8091-2742-3

Published by Paulist Press
997 Macarthur Boulevard
Mahwah, New Jersey 07430

Printed and bound in the
United States of America

CONTENTS

Prologue   1

PART ONE

1. The Spiritual Dynamic Sustaining All Ministries   3

2. Claiming What Is Owned   12

3. "Does It Make a Difference?"   26

4. In the Old Testament Yahweh Ministers   46

5. In the New Testament Jesus Ministers   65

6. In the Faithful the Holy Spirit Ministers   81

7. Discerning Basic Elements of Ministry   101

PART TWO

8. Readying the Soil for Ministry   127

9. Planting the Seed—
   Contemplative Awareness and Prayer   143

10. Watering, Weeding, Watching Developments   164

11. Harvesting the Fruit   186

Postscript—Mulching for the Future   208

Notes   211

Bibliography   214

DEDICATION

for George

PROLOGUE

What to put into a book on ministerial spirituality for lay persons engaged in voluntary ministry on the local level, how to design such a book, and why write this book were questions that challenged me before one word was penned on paper.

To answer the first question: the content of *Pilgrim in the Parish* is initially a presentation of elements that form the foundation for ministerial spirituality. These include a probing of dynamics relevant to relationship with God, and examination of the roots of ministry and spirituality—Scripture and theology—and a consideration of the environment for ministry—church.

To minister is to accept a placement in leadership, leadership that is public, leadership that is accomplished for and/or within the church. This reality necessitates at least three responses:

—learning the techniques and criteria needed in order to engage in the ministerial *task;*

—understanding how *both* ministry and spirituality are integral to church and paramount in Scripture;

—discerning whether one's image of God mirrors the God revealed in Scripture and what kind of relationship one has with the God of revelation.

In our tradition expressions of piety are immensely varied, creative and heartfelt. One hopes this dynamic will not become extinct, particularly in our technological age. Those who respond to the call to ministry, however, become accountable to the church in its people and institutional sense in a new way because, while engaged in their ministerial task, they explicitly represent the people and the institution. Implicit is a willingness to be in relationship to the God revealed in Scripture, the God

1

of Christian tradition. In this book, the reflection on the foundation for ministry and spirituality provides a substantial vantage point for reflecting on the development of a ministerial spirituality through contemplative approaches to life, ministry and prayer.

How to design a book on ministerial spirituality for lay persons engaged in grass roots voluntary ministry? In many ways the content described above has mandated the particular and diverse format the book takes. Early chapters lean toward a theological style; later chapters evoke a dynamic centered on stories. The journey that author and reader take together could be likened to a hike followed by a stroll through a meadow. But that may just be my fancy. What is not my fancy is that the content of each chapter has shaped its style.

Why bother writing a book for lay people in voluntary ministry? I was amazed at the number of people who challenged me with this question, some of them lay people who *do* voluntary ministry! Some inquirers associated me with professional ministry because of my work at the Weston School of Theology where I facilitate spiritual development for professional ministry for women and laymen. Others asked "Why bother?" from a different frame of reference. These inquirers reminded me of the parish staff person who invited me to present a workshop for particular lay ministries and I indicated that I would like to do a presentation for lectors and one for ushers. The response I received was, "Why ushers? We weren't going to bother having a workshop for ushers."

The conversation about the ushers reminded me, in turn, about the disciples saying to Jesus, "All we have is five loaves and two fishes, nothing more . . . "

In many ways voluntary ministers who are lay and located in the parish are considered the loaves and fishes of ministerial enterprise today. You might say that my motivation for writing *Pilgrim in the Parish* is the hunch that this is the hour when Jesus intends to turn those loaves and those fishes into superabundance to nourish the many waiting to be fed.

1

THE SPIRITUAL DYNAMIC SUSTAINING ALL MINISTRIES

When haven't men and women told stories? Travelers in space, coming home from their flights, tell stories. The Israelites four thousand years ago told stories in the wilderness. Jesus told stories, many stories, and I am going to begin by telling a story and commenting on a story told.

There is good reason for all this story-telling. Some things seem to make sense only when seen in the light a story sheds.

Three years ago I had an opportunity to visit New York University and observe Lee Strasberg, the originator of Method acting in the United States, teach a master class. In progress when I arrived, the class was beginning to focus attention on a young actress seated on a makeshift stage, ready to start her scene from a play. When all was silent, she delivered her first line with great emotional intensity:

"I remember my first day of school!"

At the end of the scene the actress gazed at Mr. Strasberg in hopeful expectancy.

"I remember my first day of school." He responded first by repeating her opening line. "Is that the way we start a conversation in real life?"

The actress looked puzzled.

Strasberg went on. "In real life wouldn't we be more apt to say, in a musing and quiet way, 'I remember my first day of

3

school ... ' then, gradually and unintentionally, unfold the depth of all of what that first day meant?"

Toward the end of his critique the actress asked Lee Strasberg to be more clear about how he liked the way she did the whole scene.

"Darling," he said, "my point is that you didn't *do* the scene; you gave a speech."

His reply still haunts me.

After my visit to the Strasberg Studio, walking back to the campus of New York University, I thought of Jesus' story of the two sons.

One day in the temple, Jesus told this story:

> "What is your opinion? A man had two sons. He went and said to the first, 'My boy, you go and work in the vineyard today.' He answered, 'I will not go,' but afterwards thought better of it and went. The man then went and said the same thing to the second who answered, 'Certainly, sir,' but did not go. Which of the two did the father's will?" "The first," they said. Jesus said to them, "I tell you solemnly, tax collectors and prostitutes are making their way into the kingdom of God before you. For John came to you, a pattern of true righteousness, but you did not believe him, and yet the tax collectors and prostitutes did. Even after seeing that, you refused to think better of it and believe in him (Mt 21:28-32).

Encountering a command, the father asking him to work in the vineyard, the first son responded honestly, improvised along the way, and transformed his resistant spirit into compliance.

"No, I won't work for him today"—then perhaps feelings of regret, but instead of showy apology, off to the vineyard to work. Authentically engaged, the first son may have been brash but he seems very real. In contrast, the second son was adept at giving speeches but never fulfilled the promise delivered in the speech. In my reflection, I wondered if the second son's hollow, obedient reply was what Strasberg referred to as a programmed, tape recorder response. In his critique of the scene at the studio, Strasberg claimed that once an actor's lines are memorized and internalized, an inner tape recorder can click on with the first cue, and the tongue, in an automatic reflex, can recite the lines while the performer is, mentally, a million miles away from the character and the scene and the authentic reality the playwright is trying to reveal.

As I neared Washington Square and saw its trees dwarfed by the skyscrapers on the horizon, my reflection broadened to include my own ministry and my spirituality.

"Which way am I in ministry?" I asked myself. "Do I become engaged in each scene an encounter in ministry provides? Or has role and rote turned my ministerial responses into programmed, tape recorded lines that sound like speeches?"

"Which way am I with God" I asked myself. "Am I authentically engaged with God? Or do I use prayer as an opportunity for speech-making, delivering to God a message that is stale but secure, complacent and comfortable, my mind and heart a million miles away from the vineyard God has invited me to care about?"

Although opportunities to give speeches abound in prayer, prayer that is infected by speech-making is often prayer with no vibrancy.

In preaching and in parables, Jesus illustrated his contempt for the hypocrisy behind speech-making. He was direct about the distinction he perceived between *using* a scene to pedestalize oneself to an exalted position and *doing* a scene wholeheartedly.

Ministry Versus Speech-Making

The best way to distinguish speech-making from authentic ministry is to look at some scenes that have the *potential* for ministry within them, a potential that it is up to the ministerial *person(s)* to actualize.

Nothing sounds more like speech-making than advice-giving, and my first example is the one-to-one pastoral encounter. The space around an audience of one can in an instant become a stage. And there are few among us who have not thrown the stone of advice when it was not invited. Advice-giving, a human failing not limited to particular, ill-fated persons, inhibits honest communication.

Religious education programs provide the second example of the potential for speech-making ministry. If a curriculum is too tentative and is comprised of only suggested guidelines, those engaged in the teaching ministry may use the classroom for self-proclamations that sound like speeches to the ears of the students. On the other hand, curriculum design that evokes excessive detail in lesson plans often leaves no entry for engagement with the students about their own stories and their own faith.

Another ministerial platform for speech-making that comes to mind is the occasion when ceremonial formula predominates, like eucharistic liturgy, lectoring, and leading prayer service. We have heard the phrases a hundred times over. Because of that, some of us rush through them; others of us move slowly, giving each word an artificially weighted tone that robs the text of meaning, or the narrative of its story quality. In any case, the hollowness of giving a speech disguises the import of the ritual.

My last example refers to letting speech-making, in its pride of accomplishment sense, substitute for authentic ministering by the style and thrust of activity in local parish. This syndrome came to my attention at a conference on parish life held several years ago. When a parish from Texas unveiled its schedule of weekly activities, it was as if a statue by a master had been unveiled. We stood before it in humbled awe. Week after week, night after night, there were church activities to suit every age level and to complement every interest. However, as the conference week went on, participants in my seminar seemed drawn more and more to representatives from a Hispanic community. Their parish had no razzle-dazzle program but from the stories its representatives told, one perceived that doing the scene was the heartbeat of that faith community.

What kind of ministry will be talked about in this book? In the text there are numerous examples of ministry. For the most part each example specifies a type of ministry by function, i.e., liturgical planning, nursing home visitation, social justice ministry. The point of each example, however, is often applicable to any ministry; the functions are mentioned to add a sense of specificity and to reflect the reality of the church in the United States today.

The Spirit Undergirding All of the Ministries

"Doing the scene," the cornerstone of ministerial spirituality and vibrant church, means a genuine engagement with the "real," whether, in an instance, the real is the word of God or the everyday lives of people.

A life story illustrates what doing the scene means.

Ten years ago the school where my husband and I worked closed. George was out of work for eight months. This is how our faith community, The Vineyard, responded ministerially to that reality.

A day seldom passed without a phone call from someone in the community with a good listening ear. After two months, every so often we began to receive an unsigned "thinking of you" card with money enclosed, the source of which we could never trace. Supper invitations were frequent, and accommodations for our youngest child were always available when job hunting took us out of town overnight. The priest leader suggested that my husband and he get together each week to talk and to share their needs with God.

Personal concern for us in our circumstance never flagged. For instance, one evening as I was entering the vestibule to go to Mass, I met Paul, also going to liturgy and to the meeting we were both to attend after Mass. He asked me how George was faring. I said, "Not too well!"

After Mass Paul told the chairperson for the meeting that he would be absent, and some of us, including myself, were annoyed. When I returned home, I discovered the excuse for Paul's absence—conversation and concern, along with a bottle of wine, for George.

When George found a position, it meant to our sorrow moving a hundred miles away. At a marvelous farewell party, we said goodbye to friends in faith who had become lifelines. But, of course, it wasn't farewell. Many of the members of the community were at the house the following day, taking the mop out of my hands to give the kitchen floor its final scrub, taking rubbish to the dump, loading the truck, washing windows, and doing all the other things Jesus said we should be willing to do if we desire to lead the way he served.

This is "salt of the earth" ministry. This is "love your neighbor" ministry. This is making your brother's and sister's story your own story by being authentically engaged with your brother and sister. It is the first ministry to which we are all called, and it is the criteria for what living Christian life is all about. The designated ministries, like communion distribution and evangelization, to which I will allude in subsequent pages, are designed, one hopes, to enhance the undesignated ministry of abundant concern for one another to which each baptized Christian and each Christian community are called.

Setting and Spiritual Development

Authentic engagement in ministry can happen in any church setting, from a chancery office to a confessional, from a hospital to a soup kitchen, from a pulpit to an advocacy hearing. That is not to say, however, that persons in these placements always practice ministry with this spirit of real engagement. People can lock their hearts day and night the way they lock their doors day and night, and a congregation of thirty-year vintage can still be a congregation of strangers making speeches at one another.

Regardless of setting, it is possible for *function* to so predominate in a ministry, or a collection of ministries, that the gifts people bring to the ministries never rise to life. Where both designated and undesignated ministries are barely tolerated by leadership, invitations to speech-making are boundless.

On the other hand, ministry is not always accepted by the people. When we look to Scripture, we discover that the people in Jesus' hometown preferred tried and true, tired speeches to the kind of scene-doing Jesus exemplified. We hear in Luke's gospel (Lk 4:16-30) that after listening to Jesus' preaching in the synagogue, the people Jesus grew up with "hustled him out of town." At the brow of the cliff they intended to dispose of him. What was the reaction of Jesus to this opposition? He "slipped through the crowd and walked away."

Setting is mentioned initially, here in the beginning chapter, to suggest that discerning one's ministry in relation to one's setting is part of the spiritual process involved in being a minister of God because setting is always relevant to spiritual development.

For example, a pastor once said to me, "You are a maverick. You may be good for the universal church someday, but you're no good for the parish. You have too many ideas and keep the people stirred up." The charge he leveled presented an opportunity for me to discern (a) whether to continue to "stir up" the people with ideas (not my intention), (b) whether to mute my voice and energies (not my nature), or (c) whether to shake the dust off my feet and go where I might be more welcome (not my habit).

It is good now and then to reflect on one's ministry in this manner rather than to react with only frustration or anger. It is good now and then to remember the gospel story of the two sons. In your setting do you feel as free as the first son who said, "No, I won't go?" In my story about our family crisis, Paul decided at the last moment to absent himself from the meeting to respond to a greater need. Can you be as spontaneous in your setting? Or do you feel like the second son, compelled to answer affirmatively even when your heart and mind are a million miles away from where you are being urged to participate? The motivation of the second son is never revealed. Was he afraid to voice another sentiment? Or was his primary interest in being a "people pleaser" for his own self-image?

These are a few of the questions for self-reflection I suggest in this book which is a consideration, not of the function of a particular ministry, but of the purpose *in the heart of the person engaged in ministry*. Spirituality begins here. And the claim spirituality makes is that ministry is never speech-making or "doing your own thing"; ministry is authentic engagement with the reality of God and persons.

To learn the techniques and rituals and subject matter necessary for a ministry, whether one is a lector or a deacon or a pastoral minister, is crucial. We learn these necessities, however, to make them our own, to internalize them so we can forget them in order to concentrate, in the moment never to be repeated, on the faith dynamic and the persons that ministry has at its heart.

Revealing Reality in the Moment of Ministry

For an analogy of this in drama, let's return again to the story that initiated this chapter and listen as Lee Strasberg explains to the actor the difference between making a speech and doing the scene.

A performer, he said, would know all the lines and the feelings connected to a scene. But to play the scene as the character who is *at that moment* actually living the reality of that moment, the actor would not want to leap ahead by anticipating what is to come for that would pull her concentration away from what is being revealed in the moment; she would begin to "say the lines" rather than be the character.

Saying lines is never reality. In drama the reality to be revealed by those doing the scene, the reality behind the author's words, is the heart and spirit of the play.

By responding to a call to ministry, we pledge to reveal a reality intended and authored by another, by God. Our call is to get behind "saying the lines" to the reality God is trying, through us, to reveal. We will never know the fullness of that reality in the moment of ministry; we do not need to know its fullness; we need only to be available for that reality.

If one's ministry is motivated by a solid spiritual foundation, it will seldom come across as having all the answers before the encounter even begins. Spirituality activated in an ongoing way enables lay ministers to get behind the script to the reality needing to be revealed. God will prompt us though we may not fully understand the meaning of his promptings. If we turn God's promptings into a speech, exaltation of self rather than revelation of God is apt to steal center stage.

Since Vatican II, church media and movements, theologians and the institutional church—local, diocesan, and universal—have delivered innumerable scripts, often contradictory, causing some persons in the church to lose a heartfelt sense of the reality behind the scenes. When trying to recite these kaleidoscopic lines evoked the tower of Babel, some believers became drawn by the magnet of Scripture to seek for themselves the reality behind the lines.

In the setting of Scripture they discovered that each one of us is significantly loved by God, and that each has a role significant to revealing the reality God intends, whether that be compassion for the spiritually brokenhearted or advocacy for those who are materially down and out.

A fruit of studying Scripture, reflecting on it, and praying with it was the discovery that Jesus wants "who I am" and "what I do" to become one. Spirituality, by forming my heart, shapes my gifts, the gifts I bring to a particular ministry, gifts that are intended to marry functions and enchance the spiritual reality intrinsic to the ministerial encounter. In other words, within designated ministries, like serving on the parish council or teaching religious education, there is a need for the salt of the earth flavor of undesignated ministry and the ambiance and value implied by what "lay" truly means. An abbreviated way of defining ministerial spirituality is to say it is a unity between "who I am" and "what I do" within communal caring.

To understand more deeply how Jesus reveals this reality we need to ask, "How did Jesus do the scene?" One answer can be found in the way Jesus responded to a question John the Baptist asked:

> John, who was in prison, heard what Christ was doing, and sent his own disciples to him with this message: "Are you the one who is to come or are we to expect some other?" Jesus answered, "Go and tell John what you hear and see: the blind recover their sight, the lame walk, the lepers are made clean, the deaf hear, the dead are raised to life, the poor are hearing good news—and happy the one who does not find me a stumbling block" (Mt 11:2-6).

John as a prophet expected from Jesus words and actions that would more forcefully proclaim who Jesus was. Instead Jesus practiced "salt of the earth ministry," responding in real ways to the real needs of real people. He let "who I am" and "what I do" become one; that script, as he lived it, fulfilled Isaiah's prophesy that the Messiah would give sight to the blind, enable the lame to walk, the deaf to hear. No need for making speeches; doing the scene with God would reveal the Reality called Messiah.

2

CLAIMING WHAT IS OWNED

Greater self-understanding of one's total relationship with God deepens spirituality by furthering one's understanding and trust of God, a cause for celebration in itself as we see revealed in Jesus' joy when Peter perceives him as the Messiah; Jesus responds with joy. Recognition of who Jesus is, and commitment to him, are often the pivotal moments called *conversion*. For those of us who are cradle Catholics, the maturing of our belief into conversion is seldom a striking event. More likely it is a gradual deepening of our personal relationship with God through Christ and the Holy Spirit, and a ripening of those spiritual dynamics that are part of the warp and woof of our everyday life, and consequently taken for granted. Because these dynamics are woven into the texture of our lives and selves, they are not less spiritual. As John Surette, S.J. says, "Spirituality is intimacy with God through my unique way of being in the world with others."

All this we usually tuck neatly under the cap of "faith." And in the gospel it seems that the vibrancy or the lack of faith in those he encountered was the gauge Jesus used in responding to them. The kind of faith Jesus hungered to find in Israel was *a faith open to change*. In the many healing scenes, we see Jesus affirm that faith was instrumental in evoking change—the change we called "healed." The very act of turning to Jesus indicated hope in a God of mercy. In those whom Jesus chastised he seemed to see a complacent faith, static and stubborn, infected by an adherence to form and resistant to the suppleness needed for growth. Faith that is alive bears the fruit of change.

If there is within us a vibrant faith and a readiness for change, we have already invited God, through the Spirit, to be engaged authentically with us.

12

Transformation of Faith, the Spiritual Ingredient for Ministry

Transformation is the word that best describes the activity of the Spirit within us bearing the fruit of change. Where God manifests a presence in the stories of the Old and New Testament, reactions in the midst of these encounters may differ—awe, struggle, acceptance—but the common thread is transformation within the person who has encountered God. Feeling a golden glow is not necessary for transformation nor necessarily an indication that transformation is taking place. What *is* necessary is openness to God's encounter within, a willingness to let the Spirit improvise on the immediate reality of the believer's heart. Compatability between spirituality and ministry means being in touch, in a continuing fashion, with the reality of God in the Spirit, the Spirit who improvises within in ways that evoke change, deepening the truth of self and the integrity of ministry.

Spiritual Transformation and Ministry

"Are you open to letting the Spirit improvise within you?" In a nutshell, the value of spirituality to ministry rests on the answer given to that question.

If your response is, "No, I would rather have God make speeches at me and let me pick and choose the speech to which I care to respond," then this book may inform but it will not influence. If your response is: "Well, I want the Spirit to work within me, but something holds me back," then you are in a company whose numbers are legion. Many of us *want to want* God to transform our faith; we want to have a stronger desire for a personal relationship with God; if we step back, it is often because we are afraid of the consequences of that kind of relationship. We forget that remarkable fact about our interior life: within us God is never on-stage alone. When God through the Spirit is active within us, we are also on stage.

Tyrants desire slaves, not God. God respects our freedom, and cherishes us with that freedom intact. For most of us, *experientially* knowing these theological insights is a process that takes some time, but it is a process worth the time it takes. We may wrestle with God as Jacob did; we may respond with puzzlement as Mary did to Gabriel; we may hesitate as Jesus did at Gethsemane. Or we may doubt as Thomas did after the resurrection. God created us. God understands us. These responses to encountering the Holy have been, for centuries, part of what happens when the Spirit is working within us which means *with* us.

To attempt to live a good Christian life without help from God is exhausting. Although it seems puzzling, some Christians turn a cold shoulder to the idea of having what is called a personal relationship with God. Lack of trust in themselves, as well as in God, may be the issue here.

Persons doing ministry who want to do that ministry about God but without God have inhabited the Christian church more often than we like to acknowledge or imagine.

Church ministry in this sense is something distinct from living a good Christian life. Every Christian, in a sense, represents God and the Christian church, but one who does ministry in the name of a particular church is a *public* representative of that church in a designated way, a way that implies greater responsibility. Or to put it another way, rightly or wrongly, *ministerial* attitudes and behavior evoke credit or blame in a much more visible, precise, and distinct way than simply "belonging" to the church or a parish incurs. Consequently, if a man or woman engaged in ministry prefers to have God make speeches that he or she can, will-nilly, accept or reject, the ball is always in the minister's park. This minister, resisting transformation of faith, is a high-risk representative for parish or church.

Spirituality is essential to ministry. The person doing ministry, whether it be the ministry of teaching or of lectoring or of pastoral leadership, has an inner spiritual framework that influences that ministry no matter how meager the influence. What kind of mutuality there is between God and the ministerial person is a question this book addresses, a question at the heart of spirituality.

Ministries, whether they be religious education or home visitation or eucharistic distribution, are intended to facilitate the transforming movement of the Spirit in believers. As lay ministers we are called to be persons who help facilitate that transforming movement. Unless we ourselves are willing to be transformed, how dare we help facilitate, by our engagement in ministry, the transforming movement of the Spirit in others?

To realize that the Spirit wants to be close to our lives and transform our hearts is awesome. Intimate is the word usually chosen to describe a relationship such as this. And we know, from our experience of being in the world with others, that intimacy in relationship to these others can be akin to playing with fire—one never knows what may be enkindled. Paradoxically, intimacy with God (through my unique way of being with others), and the transformation born of that intimacy, promises that one's foundation for ministry is built on rock not sand.

Rationally we understand this, but psychically we resist. We keep backing away from intimacy and transformation because to step forward is risk. Few of us are foolhardy enough to embrace risk. It *is* awesome to say that God is that close to me and my life—to say that Jesus is that real, as real to me in my life as he was to Mary Magdalene and to John, as real and near to my community as he was to the original disciples. Transformation means upheaval, and who among us does not have at least a tinge of the Pharisee's zeal for order and correctness and continuity? Companions in this process can be consoling.

Models of Resistance

With this challenge before us, let's look at two models of resistance and see if what Alice or Matt has chosen is what we prefer.

Involved in three ministries within her parish, Alice is also a member of a diocesan commission. Not only too busy to pay any attention to her spiritual life, Alice is motivated by an optimism that has as its source quid pro quo—the more I do good works for God, the more good he will do for me. Whether there is evidence for God's good works depending on Alice's good works, Alice has not taken the time to discern.

On the other hand, Matt feels that if he does too much ministry he may get in over his head. His saying that refers to becoming too busy to see the woods for the trees, but it also applies to his sense that a real commitment to ministry implies a commitment to Christ that could upset the applecart in ways he can't articulate. Restraint insures that the reins on real change stay firmly in Matt's hands.

Sometimes it takes stories like these for us to realize that spirituality is not a marginal element in regard to ministry.

As ministers we have a choice about whether to devote time and energy to a personal relationship with God, but choosing *against* a personal relationship with God presents another kind of risk for one's Christian life in general as well as for the ministerial life of the church.

The activity of the internal life of the church *is* ministry; the fabric of church life, in many ways, is woven by the quality of its ministry, quality that rests in part on spiritual maturity, quality that often models the attitudes the rest of the community adopts. A church civil service embodied by lay ministers is on its way if this internal activity is accomplished by persons who resist the reality of the Spirit working within them, and within the totality of a parish. If dioceses are composed of parishes along this line, a gigantic church civil service is in the works.

On the other hand, a vibrant community may be in the process of creation if this internal activity is accomplished by persons open to God's authentic engagement within them. And a vibrant church may be coming alive if dioceses are composed of parishes of this sort. (The willingness to participate in evaluative processes done by persons with no self-interest in the ministry, the parish, or diocese is, of course, an indication that the kind of faith that risks change is "at hand.")

Elements of Spirituality Significant to Ministry

Most believers who have taken the risk and welcomed intimacy with God through their unique way of being in the world with others testify to being more happy, more courageous, and more peaceful within. As for God demanding some unusual manifestation of faith, I know of only one person who felt that spirituality led him to fly to India to be with Mother Teresa— and he embarked on that journey to convert her to his prayer style!

In talking about the significance of spirituality for the lay persons engaged in voluntary ministry, it is helpful to keep four elements in mind.

First, for every journey we make in life, acquiring provisions is essential. In a like fashion, letting oneself be drawn into a deeper life with God is acquiring provision for ministry, and for living a Christian life, by acquiring the love, joy, courage, and peace that are signs of transformed faith.

Second, by taking time for after-the-fact reflection on ministerial experiences in contemplative prayer, a person begins to recognize some of the religious experiences already happening in his or her life. One of the most poignant facts about faith life today is that believers often have a range of religious experience that never comes to the level of consciousness where it can be recognized as *religious* experience. In other words, your spiritual life is not something that might happen next year when you join a prayer group, or next week when you finish this book and begin to experiment with its suggestions; your spiritual life is what is happening right now! Religious experience has been happening to each of us for a long time; what we need are the tools to recognize it, the magnifying glass that will help us notice how the Spirit *is* improvising within us.

The third and fourth elements relate even more directly to "being in the world with others." As your spiritual dimensions mature, you may be drawn to greater action or witness—"upsetting the applecart," which was what Matt feared in an earlier example. When the motivation for this comes, however, from the interrelationship between spirituality and ministry, *desire* draws the person to action and witness. Without the involvement of the spiritual dimension linking us to others and to God, conscience alone can be the motivating source. Duty, not desire, then becomes the catalyst for the action or witness. When one fails and guilt inevitably emerges, the upset applecart is feeling torn within. Duty evokes quid pro quo which is almost always ineffectual. Action and witness that is a fruit of spirituality and ministry emerges from the vibrancy of inner transformation enabled by God.

When participation in ministry is accompanied by a maturing of spirituality, the believer begins to savor the relatedness between persons and among ministries in his or her local setting. A greater appreciation for Paul's insight—the upbuilding of the church community—and a more concrete sense of being part of that upbuilding often result.

Detours Along the Road

Confusion about spirituality leads to resistance.

When Lorraine, who is a lector, prays, "nothing happens." When Lorraine's sister-in-law prays, a great deal "happens." Lorraine gave prayer a good try, concluding that spirituality may be for others but it's not for her.

Stan enjoyed the prayer group he was in at St. Martin's parish where he often helped with the Catholic Charities appeal. A job transfer meant a new location and a new parish, one where there was no prayer group or opportunity for ministry. On his own Stan found some puzzling things happening when he prayed. When he tried to explain this to persons who could help him understand himself spiritually, he felt tongue-tied. He's beginning to feel it's not worth trying.

Michelle noticed that in addition to enjoying her term on the parish council, she was beginning to like reading books on spirituality. Her curiosity led to a desire to develop more maturity in regard to spiritual matters until a co-member to whom she mentioned this tried to convince Michelle that his way of meditation was the one and only path for her to follow. Finding him tiresome, Michelle also began to find her interest in spirituality waning.

Spirituality sometimes has a bad name. There are many reasons for this as the examples above illustrate. You may feel intimidated by other people's spirituality. Spirituality seems elusive, and religious experiences, including prayer experiences, are often not easy to talk about. Becoming resistant when "friends" eagerly try to impose their brand of spirituality on others is common. Spirituality that strikes an observer as phony or showy is not inviting.

The identity between spirituality and intimacy naturally evokes self-consciousness in regard to sharing one's own spiritual experiences with others. Believers who are eager and ready for further development are easily hurt by people who lack sensitivity. What is sad about the above experiences, experiences that are very common in our church and culture, is how easy it is to become inhibited about initiating new efforts regarding spirituality and how difficult it is to appreciate the spiritual dynamics *already active within ourselves.*

Spiritual Dynamics—Claiming What Is Already Yours

God's creation of the world is the first spiritual dynamic to which we can lay claim. Believers are called to affirm that the universe was created by God, that is, by One radically different from ourselves, who now upholds the activity of the universe. Another way of putting this is to say that God created the world, and that God sustains our world, and us within it, whether we have the graciousness to celebrate this as spiritual or not!

A large, silk-screened print on the wall of a bank in Boston depicts Noah's ark, filled to the brim with familiar animals. What is unusual about the depiction is the ocean. It teems with pairs of fish and whales, accompanying the ark and suggesting a less than lonesome voyage. The print is my favorite reminder that God created a universe for us to cherish as a home.

Every Sunday morning in churches across the land, lay persons like Alice and Lorraine, Stan, Matt, and Michelle engage in the ministries of lectoring, ushering, music, eucharistic distribution, and religious education. Within each of these persons, spiritual dynamics like the above—God's gift of creation as our home—are brought to the particular ministry in which the lay minister is engaged. To deepen an awareness of our legitimate claim to these dynamics, we will reflect on them.

You were created by God. I was created by God. The second fundamental spiritual dynamic is the fact that we were created by God. Life experience and the culture surrounding us has, at times, worked in tandem with the gifts and talents that originated in our God-empowered createdness. Because the development of these gifts and talents happens over a span of time, they sometimes become taken for granted and the Source is forgotten. A deliberate reflection on one's createdness and giftedness is often needed for a recognition that this dynamic is a spiritual fact, not only an impersonal theological truth.

A third spiritual dynamic we bring to ministry is our ability to love and the plenitude of instances when we have loved, when we have struggled to respond with our hearts and minds and spirits to God, and when we have cherished neighbor as much as self. Loving relates us to God, but the truth of love as a spiritual dynamic does not depend on whether we do or do not *consciously* relate our experiences of loving others to God. As Karl Rahner puts it:

> This (kind of) experience of God is not the privilege of the individual "mystic," but is present in every man and woman *though the process of reflecting on it* varies greatly from one individual to another in terms of force and clarity.[1] (Emphasis mine)

So whether we have recognized them or not, those innumerable times when in our hearts we have loved, particularly the stranger and the one in need, form within us a spiritual dynamic that binds us to God.

Our participation in various communities also has spiritual ramifications. For example, ongoing fidelity within marriage and family (between spouses, between offspring and parents, between parents and offspring) renews again and again our unity with God.

Since baptism, each of us has been incorporated into the community of the church. Whether we celebrate this or not, the spiritual ties remain intact, for the reality of this bonding depends less on the vagaries of our mood than on the overall commitment of the will and heart, unless, with clear mind and uncluttered conscience, we sever that tie. When we participate in our civic community by reflecting on the values of others and by sharing with them the values we cherish, another spiritual link with God, through community, is forged.

The spiritual dynamic that most commonly comes to mind perhaps is the sacramental life that enriches the faith of most

Catholic Christians. Participation in the sacraments continually renews bonds with God and with church community, the setting for the celebration of the sacraments. Baptism, confirmation, marriage, reconciliation, and the sacrament of the sick—each of these draws us into unity with God at milestones in our human life. To complete the tapestry, we are gifted with the Eucharist, the graciously available bread and wine, body and blood of the Lord, that tells us that each day or each week is a milestone when one lives his or her life with God.

Although other dynamics could be described, I will end this inventory of spritual dynamics with Mission to the World, the call from Christ to the men and women of the church to renew with depth and value the society and world in which they live. By raising families in a caring way, by hospitality to neighbor and stranger, by bringing integrity, honesty, and responsibility to the workplace, by participating in efforts of justice and peace, by facing in so many ways the difficult challenges of life with a spirit of courage, Christian men and women renew, day after day, week after week, their spiritual bond with their God—Creator, Redeemer, and Transformer.

Lay ministers are particular persons making particular responses *within a spiritual people.* Although ministry can be an opportunity to develop further our already-in-existence spirituality, no one in the church "gets spiritual" solely by becoming a minister.

Our response to the call to ministry unfolds from vibrant spiritual links already forged with God. These dynamics become the spiritual foundation for ministry, a foundation with many layers resembling what geologists tell us about the earth, a foundation started long before we knew what the word ministry meant.

Short-Circuiting Spiritual Vitality

Our technological age and the pace of our times spawn tendencies that often depreciate more than appreciate. In any era that slights what is not experiential, during times when the pace of life leaves little time to *reflect* on what has been lived, it is easy to lose sight of the fundamental spiritual dynamics that are ours to claim.

Ministry evokes the call to spiritual maturity and, consequently, to full adulthood in the Church, a call to forsake any fixation on programs, including religious education of children, or any obsession with the human foibles of fellow parishioners or priests or pastor.

The emergence of lay ministers in a local setting causing a separating the sheep from the goats phenomenon, a syndrome that lifts lay ministers to a realm above the rest of the lay people in a setting, evokes an elitism that has no rightful place among ministers or among ministries.

As the following story illustrates, insufficient understanding sometimes also short-circuits ministry, and even within ministries unfortunate distinctions are sometimes made.

One evening at choir rehearsal during Lent, John, a choir member with an outstanding tenor voice, informed the director that he would not be able to sing at the Easter Vigil. The choir director expressed her dismay and asked if John planned to be out of town for the holiday. "Oh, no," he replied. "I'll be right here at Mass. But I'm a eucharistic minister for the Vigil, so I won't be able to sing, as I want to concentrate on that ministry."

In the discussion that ensued, John was adamant about the deeper spiritual value that communion distribution has over contributing to the music ministry at the Vigil. Compared to the opportunity to help serve at the altar, the spiritual needs of the parish community and his God-given gift of a gracious voice were minor. This distinction was a *spiritual* perspective John brought to ministry, but whether John came to his discernment about the Easter Vigil through a conscious reflection within his personal relationship with God or whether it was an "automatic" reflex from years of cultural influence within the church we don't know.

Education in what it means to be spiritual as well as what it means to be ministerial, and education in what it means to be a member of a faith community, can help rectify the kind of imbalance of priorities that the onset of lay ministries sometimes activates.

Though we who are Catholic Christians nourish our faith through spiritual dynamics, we may not perceive particular dynamics with clarity. As Catholic believers a personal relationship with God can be a priority for our life of faith, for our tradition is rich with the means to enable this. Our God-person relationship is enhanced by the spiritual dynamics described in this chapter. Affirming this personal relationship need not isolate us, for spiritual vitality is the fundamental bond we share with our sisters and brothers in Christ. We are called to celebrate the stories that exemplify relationship rather than division, like the story of Fred Hanson and Joe Petrelli who are next-door neighbors and lifelong members of St. Ambrose parish. Both express with fullness the spiritual dynamics of commitment to the women they married and to the children born of their marriages. Both work honestly and responsibly for the same firm. Fred has been particularly active in union affairs. Though Joe is also a union member, his activity beyond family and work has centered on the parish where he has served as a sacristan and a religious education teacher. Good and better and best are distinctions Fred and Joe make only about who has the winning hand of poker on a Friday night.

The Circumference of Spirituality

Before a word about prayer is said, before a word of prayer is uttered, we have entered the realm of spirituality. Creation, the bestowal of gifts and talents, providence, love, community, sacramental life and mission connect us to God. Though you may not have recognized or experienced all of these within your consciousness as *personal spiritual "events,"* though you may have let them fall into the taken-for-granted category, now is the time to reflect on this strong interior foundation that is your "dowry" for ministry and prayer. Without reflection you may cheat yourself and see, for example, your civic involvements as only secular in nature, or you may credit your gifts and talents solely to genes and educational institutions.

To be human is to be spirited; it is not something we "get" at baptism. Baptism initiates us as spirited beings into Christian community. Our subsequent life in the church nourishes that spiritedness.

Consequently, when I respond to the call to a particular ministry, I respond because my spirit has heard that call and I bring to ministry whatever fullness of spirit has deepened my faith. Because of this, as I train for ministry and as I minister, a dialogue takes place between the spirited person I am and the ministry in which I am engaged.

There are four potential settings for "who I am" to initiate dialogue with "what I do":

- the personal level
- the parish or community level
- the universal church level
- the mission level

On the personal level I may begin to sense how my ministry is affecting my faith life. For example, if I am a lector I may notice that the Spirit through my faith is drawing me to cherish Scripture.

On the parish level, I may begin to notice that my ministry is bringing me in contact with other lay ministers. Because of this I am developing an appreciation for community leadership that is collaborative. My faith responds by evoking a vision of church as community.

On the universal level, I may find myself becoming more aware of how other churches minister to their members. For example, if I am a hospital visitor I notice that pastoral health care ministers from other denominations visit the sick and pray with them more easily than I do. I discover that I can learn from those in other religious traditions.

On the mission level, I may find myself, as I make sandwiches at home for the soup kitchen, reflecting on famine in Africa. And I move from including that concern in family Lenten prayers to suggesting ways that we, as family, can respond to the needs of God's people in Africa.

In each of these four instances, the lay minister is expanding his or her awareness of how he or she is a minister of God. In the first chapter, readers were reminded that ministers are called to reveal a reality intended and authored by another, by God. Awareness of God and awareness of his ministry bring hope and life to one's own ministry. For that reason, in the next chapters we will consider first awareness of self and God in prayer, then awareness of God's ministry.

This reflection is suggested to help the lay minister discern a response to the following question: "Whose minister am I?" If one is involved in ministry "to help Father out" or "to make the parish better," one's self-image regarding ministry may be "I'm Fr. O'Brien's minister" or "I'm Sacred Heart's minister." In this dynamic God may have a peripheral role.

To answer "Whose minister am I?" we ask first: "Who is God?" and "Who am I?" in prayer.

3

"DOES IT MAKE A DIFFERENCE?"

Two dynamics ring out loud and clear in the New Testament: followers of Jesus don't engage in ministry and/or mission without praying. Followers of Jesus don't pray without engaging in ministry and/or mission.

An unfortunate tendency in some settings within the Church in recent years is to short-change the ministry and/or mission. In other settings there appears to be a tendency to short-circuit personal relationship with God, enhanced by prayer. Mission, ministry, even asceticism, I feel, are the cart not the horse. Although each is a constitutive manifestation of Christian life, they bear fruit that is lasting and abundant when they emerge from an acceptance of the initial invitation to ongoing, relational intimacy with God through the Spirit and Jesus.

The latter dynamic lets the Spirit work interiorly, enabling us, as disciples, to do the scene to which we are called in the world. Our willingness to live out the intentions that go with discipleship ratifies our acknowledgement that our commitment is to God.

The original disciples went on mission only after a time of companionship with Jesus. As mentioned earlier, coming to know Jesus through the New Testament and responding in a heartfelt way often becomes the adult turning point called conversion. Trying to accomplish perfection or ministry or mission to the world without a vibrant spiritual life, sustained by prayer, is like trying to lift water from a well gone dry. To engage in ministry or mission without God's companionship can be to opt for the withered tree.

What is described in the above paragraphs may, at present, be more goal than realization; consequently, questions like the three following fundamental inquiries about faith provide a format for self-reflection on prayer, an activity that is the initial stage for any valid consideration of one's spiritual development:

Does it make a difference who God is for me in prayer?

Does it make a difference who I am when I come to pray?

Does what I pray about make a difference?

Your own response to each query may help you to clarify your attitudes regarding prayer and spirituality. To enhance this, you may want to read the following sections more slowly than usual, replying to the questions asked and reacting to the suggestions offered, remembering that by engaging in each exercise you are ministering to yourself.

Does It Make a Difference Who God Is for Me in Prayer?

Yesterday I tried to buy a baptism card for a six month old baby. What I actually did buy was a kind of "welcome to the world" card, secular in nature. There were baptism cards on the rack. Those few that referred to God referred to a divine being far distant in the sky. Most referred simply to "Above." "Above," it was hoped, would shine down graciously upon the newborn babe. Perhaps "Above" was substituted for God to hurt no one's feelings. Mine were hurt. It made a difference to me how God was identified. Hallmark may care enough to send the very best, but does it care enough to be theologically apt? Better a secular card on which I can imprint my own faith sentiment.

On the way back from the card store, it came to me that I may be a minority. Many, many card buyers probably prefer to think of God as a Vague Above Figure, shining down like the sun, caring without challenging.

The Psalmists

When it comes to *prayer,* does it really make a difference who God is for me in prayer? It certainly made a difference to the psalmists, and because as Christians we believe in a God revealed in Scripture rather than in a Vague Above Figure, it may prove interesting, and surprising, to begin with the psalmists.

As you read the following three psalms, notice the contrasts between the image of God presented by each psalmist.

Psalm 144
Praise the Lord, my protector!
He trains me for battle and prepares me for war,
He is my protector and defender,
my shelter and my savior,
in whom I trust for safety.
He subdues the nations under me. . . .

Psalm 88
Lord, I call to you for help;
every morning I pray to you.
Why do you reject me, Lord?
Why do you turn away from me?
Ever since I was young,
I have suffered and been near death;
I am worn out from the burden of your punishments.
Your furious anger crushed me;
Your terrible attacks destroy me.

Psalm 139
Lord, you have examined me and you know me. . . .
Even before I speak
you already know what I will say.
You are all around me on every side;
you protect me with your power.
Your knowledge of me is too deep;
it is beyond my understanding.
Examine me, O God, and know my mind,
test me and discover my thoughts.
Find out if there is any evil in me
and guide me in the everlasting way.

To these three psalmists did it make a difference who God was for them? Each certainly had a different image of God. On the other hand, the psalmists had three things in common:

Each contemplated God.

Each had a vivid image of God as active in his own history.

Each prayed openly with a wealth of feeling.

The one who prays Psalm 144 seemed to see God as general of an army doing battle at the front line. God is on the side of the one at prayer—sheltering, saving, protecting, defending, and subduing enemy armies for the sake of the one who offers praise. It strikes me as an arrogant stance for one who prays.

In the second example, Psalm 88, the image is reversed. For this psalmist, God is like a general acting *against* the one who begs for help, crushing him like an enemy, punishing him as if he were a captive, attacking and destroying the one who, paradoxically, is still willing to pray to his adversary.

The one who prays Psalm 139 presents an image that is less militaristic and more attractive and fascinating to me than the others. As portrayed in this psalm, God is all-knowing, powerful, omnipresent (you are all around me on every side), yet mystery (your knowledge is beyond my understanding). The transcendence of God seems overwhelming, yet the psalmist is not cowed. The one at prayer cherishes intimacy. The greatness of God does not inhibit the desire to be relational—examine me, know me, test me, discover me, guide me. God is awesome, yet close and caring.

Perhaps the three psalmists were the same psalmist during different seasons. That is the way some of us humans are. During Lent we may perceive God differently than we do in midsummer on vacation. Does that make a difference in the way we pray?

Let's look at it another way. How would you reply to an inquiring photographer, stopping you on the street one Thursday afternoon and asking, "Who was God like for you last Sunday?"

"You did pray at church on Sunday?"

"Well, yeah—I did pray. It's a little difficult to describe who God was for me when I prayed though."

If that answer is similar to your answer, you are not alone. For most of us God is elusive; a ready description of God is not on the tip of our tongues as it seemed to be for the psalmists. We can learn from the psalmists, however. Coming to greater clarity about who God is for us in prayer can make our prayer more vibrant. And vibrancy certainly characterizes the prayer of the psalmists. The person praying Psalm 88 sounds as if he hated God, yet he was able to express his feelings in a very real way. The psalmist did not become crippled, mute, or inattentive as some of us today are when we try to pray.

Fr. William Barry, S.J. and Fr. William Connelly, S.J. point us in the right direction when they say, "Relationships develop only when the persons involved pay attention to one another." The authors go on to explain why this is not an easy matter:

> We make an assumption based on Christian tradition that God is taking his part in the relationship, is paying attention to (the one praying), is looking at and listening to him or her. The (person praying), however, if the relationship is to develop, must also pay attention to the Lord. This is not a complex matter, but it is not necessarily easy either. There is first of all, the difficulty we human beings have in paying attention to anyone else. Then there is the difficulty of paying attention to the invisible, mysterious, and all-powerful God.[1]

Who Was God for Jesus?

Reflecting on Scripture can sometimes enable us to perceive more clearly who God is for Jesus in prayer. And a response to the question is more available than we might suppose. It made such a difference to Jesus that, in his personal prayer, he did not seem to use the traditional names for God such as King of the universe; instead, he addressed his prayer to Abba (dearest father).

This "leap of faith" was not only new, it was original in a startling way. In the Jewish religion, the name of God, Yahweh, represented the being of God so it was not pronounced in reading or prayer. (So elevated was God considered to be that in

Matthew's Jewish-Christian community the phrase kingdom of heaven was used rather than kingdom of God.)

Jesus, on the other hand, not only referred to God by the rarely used title of Father (occurring only twice in Old Testament scriptures) but he also uses in his address the intimacy of an endearment—dearest father. It would seem that in contemplating God, Jesus perceived God in roles not identical to what he had been taught and was free interiorly to make this momentous shift.

Consequently, Christian believers are called to notice the One to whom Jesus prayed and the active qualities portrayed in the references Jesus made to the Father. In the parables of the lost sheep, the lost coin and the lost son, we sense the desire in God for return and fidelity—a desire so deep that God searches and welcomes and orders celebration when what is lost is found (Lk 15:7, 10, 22).

In Luke 12:22-32 and in Matthew we hear Jesus tell us that God cares for the least significant in the animal and plant kingdoms—that God clothes the grass and the flowers of the field, that the Father knows our needs and will respond to them when we as disciples set our hearts on the kingdom which he has given to the disciples. In God's kingdom the greatest are those who make themselves as little as children (Mt 18:4), and it is to simple and faithful persons that God reveals what he hides from the learned and clever (Lk 10:21-22).

But we also hear, in the parables especially, that God in his kingdom is like a master who, out of pity, cancelled the debt of a servant. The servant, not learning from this example, throttles one who owed *him* money. When the master hears of it, he angrily hands the servant "over to the torturers till he should pay all his debt. And that is how my heavenly Father will deal with you unless you each forgive your brother from your heart" (Mt 18:23-35).

These descriptions are the bare bones of what one can mine from Scripture. Spending time noticing what Jesus draws attention to regarding the Father can effectively enhance clarity so long as one maintains an awareness that God is much more than the sum of any put-together parts, that God is beyond what we can fully image yet closer to us than our imagination can credit.

Jesus, by sharing who God is for him, fills in the bare out-
line that "naming" supplies, and the "Who" becomes One who
wants to forgive us and wants to find a forgiving heart in us, One
who wants to embrace and wants to respond to our needs, One
who has power, One who is decisive.

Images from the Past

If the One to whom we pray seems somewhat different from
the ministerial God suggested by Scripture, it should not be too
surprising considering the way images have been formed within
us. Parents and other relatives, perhaps unfamiliar with Scripture, contributed to the imprinting of many images that remain
with us. Morality training and sacramental preparation may
have been the extent of our early religious education. The
preaching to which we were exposed probably varied consider-
ably. And our devotional life may not have been grounded in
Scripture. One thing as sure as taxes is that most of us who are
Catholic received imput which we passively digested rather than
contemplated, challenged, or questioned.

Because of this, in discerning the Who to whom I pray, it
can be helpful to reflect on who God was for me when I was a
child or an adolescent or a young adult. On inviting a group of
lay ministers to do this, I found interesting and varied responses.
The first to share, Martha, spoke in a voice that trembled as she
recounted how as a college student God seemed to her so cold
and distant that she felt anxious every time she tried to pray.

"I just felt flat," said Larry. "God was always explained to
me in such abstract terms that he always seemed wishy-washy
and vague."

"Not to me!" Dot chimed in. "When I was a little girl, after
I said my night prayers, I would settle near the wall by my bed
and make room for Jesus to sit with me. I always went to sleep
embraced by the sweet and warm presence of God."

These three Catholic adults experienced God in ways
almost as varied as the three psalmists referred to earlier. The
diversity in imaging God expanded as others in the parish hall
shared early images of God. When the group was invited to
share who God is for them in recent prayer experiences, two

words came up again and again: close and caring. Most of the lay ministers had come to experience what Dot has savored since childhood—that God can be experienced as personal, tangible, loving and ministerial.

Whom Can I Trust?

Does it make a difference who God is for me when I pray? The last perspective on this question is from the vantage of analogy to life experience.

Isn't it true that in everyday life, when we want to share part of our more secret self, we are quite careful of whom we select for this confidentiality? We may say, "I won't tell *her* because if I do, the whole family will know it by next week." And we sometimes say, "If I tell *him,* he'll just belittle it and make fun of me."

"Whom can I trust?"

This is a deep and sobering question that faces us in our everyday life. It is equally significant when addressed to our spiritual life, for the quality of our prayer depends, in great part, on whether we feel that we can be trusting and intimate with the One with whom our heart shares.

In family, neighborhood, workplace, and church community, we share if we feel we can trust. It is no different when we come to God in prayer. When one lay minister looked back to her prayer as a young adult, a vivid memory emerged. It was of an experience that happened late one Saturday afternoon in winter:

> When I entered the church, the darkness comforted my heart grown weary from carrying an unspoken desire. I walked down the aisle toward the Mary altar, aglow with candlelight. Before I reached the altar rail, tears were streaming down my face. Kneeling, I begged Mary to heed the ache in my heart and do her part to grant my request. I can't remember the statue of Mary in the niche above the altar but I do remember the light from the candles, lit in plea perhaps as fervent as mine. I could share my heart openly with Mary because I trusted her. And I trusted that she not only could speak to my God who was too awesome for me to address, but she could also have her way with him. Whether she took notice

of me and my plight, I didn't know. Though I dearly wanted a benevolent response to my need, what counted at the moment was that I had voiced it, openly—to myself—as I voiced it to her. With Mary I could risk revealing myself to myself as well as to God.

Sometimes we don't know our own hearts until we come to prayer. Today this woman comes before God as she once came before Mary, and she comes with the conviction that God will notice her. If we fear God, we make him into a watchdog protecting divine purity and property *against* us. If we resent God, we will never give the Spirit entry into our hearts, never allow the Spirit to do the scene within us with us. If we are ministers who are bitter or who mistrust God, our ministry has started off on a poor footing. (Though it may not be easy to do, the secret to resolving this dilemma is to tell God how much I mistrust or resent God *with the courage of the psalmist!*)

If we believe that God ministers to us, then we may also acknowledge that he contemplates us to discover what needs to be revealed, what needs to be nourished, what needs to be taught, what needs to be welcomed hospitably, what needs to be forgiven to further fidelity.

If we believe that God ministers to us, we are more apt to say through our ministries, "God has ministered to me, so he will minister to you"—drawing the persons to God and community rather than to self.

If we trust God, then our needs and his desires for us can enter into dialogue. What is the nature of that dialogue? Our ordinary life experience tells us that where we discover trust we reveal the secrets hidden in the deeper self. Where God finds trust, God also reveals.

For me, it *does* make a difference who God is for me when I pray. It makes a difference if God is One whom I can *trust*. Trust evokes alignment that exorcises speech-making and evokes engagement with reality, not necessarily as a dialogue of words or thoughts or even shared feelings, but as a dialogue of *revealing* between Beloved and beloved, beloved and Beloved.

Does It Make a Difference Who I Am
When I Come to God in Prayer?

As you may have guessed, while answering our first question we moved into answering this question. Who I am when I come to prayer depends in part on whom I believe I will meet when I do pray. Martha, in our earlier example, felt that God was cold and distant and that influenced how she came to prayer. Toward the end of the last section, an example of trust that a believer had in Mary enabled her to come to prayer with an open heart.

Interestingly enough, it seems that when men and women perceive God to be as Mary was perceived—close and caring— their attitudes toward prayer change. Some Christians find that same trust at work when they come to Jesus in prayer.

A Scripture scholar once identified Jesus as the Parable of God. By that he meant that in Jesus we hear the story of God and we encounter God with all of his primary qualities as perfectly revealed as they are able to be in one who shares the fullness of humanity. To care about Jesus is to care about what Jesus cares about. His readiness to point beyond himself to the Father and the Spirit challenges us, in our devotion, to contemplate where Jesus draws our attention.

A friend once said, "You ask, 'Who am I in prayer?' I ask, 'Which me do I bring to prayer?'"

She has a point. If the "me" I bring to prayer is the one who dashes to prayer, always distracted and busy within, then in my heart of hearts, I know that this "who" is the superficial me, not the most real me. The superficial me, meeting the real God, somehow does not seem to work. To notice the real God calls for me being the real me.

When I come to prayer hyperactive within, I prefer God's answering service where I can leave a message and tune in later for a response. At the time of prayer, I really don't want to listen; I want to get prayer off my laundry list of things to do. The opposite extreme is when I feel that I have to get dressed up in my Sunday best to come to God in prayer. Although Sunday best is how I may go to Mass, it is not the best outfit to wear for everyday or crisis prayer. If there is such a thing as readying oneself for prayer—and I believe there is—then instead of the upward mobility represented by Sunday best, I suggest the downward mobility of jeans or shorts or apron as the inner attire that encourages the real me *to reveal* the real self in prayer.

It took me a while to learn this, and I still remember the night the lesson hit home.

> The dining room in our apartment was large enough to house the stereo and a studio couch. About nine in the evening, I settled onto the couch, hoping to let music lead me into prayer. Then the table confronted me. In our home, I cook and others do the dishes. And cook I had that night— from soup to nuts including barbequed spare ribs. There they were—the now meatless sauced ribs, scattered on plates and platters, searing my eyes. As the reality of life sometimes insists, the special dinner had evoked tension rather than peace. At the end of the dinner one after another in the family had slammed, or slipped, out of the house, leaving me in the company of plates with greasy ribs and glasses with rouged fingerprints. I groaned, knowing I would have to attack the table before coming to God in prayer, for surely I couldn't invite the Lord into the mess the dining room was. Exhausted and frustrated, I opened the Bible to find a verse to strengthen me for the task ahead. What I found without looking was Jesus healing the leper. After reading the passage, I smiled. If Jesus was about the business of healing lepers by touching them, then rib bones and grease prints wouldn't keep Jesus from coming to me here in the dining room. I put on the headphones, turned on the stereo, and collapsed into the arms of the Lord who listened to my sighs and groans, responding to me as I sensed that my chores for the evening were over. In no way was that table *my* responsibility no matter who was coming to visit!

From this experience I learned something about who God wants me to be in prayer. Later, this lesson evolved, at workshops for parish lay ministers, into a "Guess Who's Coming to Dinner?"exercise to help people discern who God may want them to be in prayer.

Guess Who's Coming to Dinner?

"Guess Who's Coming to Dinner?" is a reflective exercise in which the reader is invited to be a participant. In each of the six scenarios described below, imagine yourself finding a typed note by your front door saying, "Please excuse my manners, but I find myself in your neighborhood and would like to stop by for dinner." Beneath the message are illegibly scribbled initials.

Later, you hear the doorbell ring. You go to the door, open it, and greet the person who is coming, unexpectedly, for dinner.

Sense your reactions to each surprise visitor.

The first visitor is a good friend with whom you have happily and honestly shared many experiences and stories. What do you say? What do you feel?

The second visitor is a parish acquaintance of good repute. With the parishioner is a recently released inmate from the county jail. The parishioner talks about a project of finding temporary room and board for released prisoners. What do you say? What do you feel?

The third visitor is a person with whom you have socialized on occasion. This person is a notorious talker and most of the talk is tiresome complaint. What do you say? What do you feel?

The fourth visitor is the pastor from your church. What do you say? What do you feel?

The fifth visitor is a relative with good news. You have won a trip to your heart's desire in a local lottery. What do you say? What do you feel?

The sixth visitor is the tiresome complainer who, this time, seems stunned and mumbles something about a terrible accident. "I can't bear the loss! I can't stand it!" is all you can clearly hear. What do you say? What do you feel?

If you were honest with yourself in doing this exercise, then you have some insight into yourself—your receptivity, your ability to tolerate surprise and change, the coherence between what you say and what you feel. The latter is particularly relevant to "who I am when I come to prayer."

Now let's try it again with a different twist. Invite your image of *God* to take your place greeting the person at the door. Evaluate what you feel God would say and what you think God would feel greeting: your good friend, the parish acquaintance with the released prisoner, the notorious talker, your pastor, your relative with good news, the complainer in trauma.

When I do this workshop with parish lay ministers, the overwhelming response, of course, is that God invites everyone to the banquet table and particularly welcomes those whom we might be most eager to turn away. On another level, we might say God sees *each of us* as the person in the last example. God may perceive us as sometimes being tiresome complainers and as suffering a loss—as a victim of an accident. Some call this accident original sin; some call it the human condition; Jesus, on the way of the cross, called it "they know not what they do"; St. Paul suggests that we are strongest when we are most caught up in our weakness, for that is when we can know that the Searcher of lost sheep is pursuing us.

A third way to do this exercise is to imagine God leaving the note and coming to visit and staying for supper—or to imagine the Spirit in those who come—or to imagine Jesus with each of them. Once again: What would you say? What would you feel?

The lesson in all this is that it makes *no* difference "who I am" when I come to God in prayer. My willingness to turn to God and to want fidelity means my becoming part of the company coming to dinner whom God welcomes with generous embrace.

Reflecting on your choices in these exercises may shed light on who you and God are together. If I image God as bringing good news, then ultimately my trust will deepen as will my readiness to listen to him. This encourages the real me to come to God in prayer. If I image God as a close yet honest friend, then that makes a difference in who I am in prayer. If I also image God with the released prisoner, my response may be a shade different than if I image God as only *my* good friend. If I image God as only a tiresome complainer—I've got a long way to go!

The Responses of Jesus

Another way to reflect on the question "Does it make a difference who I am in prayer?" is to consider the responses Jesus made to those who, in a variety of settings and ways, came to him and communicated with him. How he responded lends some insight into how God might respond to us and encourage us to be in prayer.

For example, from the Canaanite woman who wouldn't accept Jesus' rejection of her request, who outwitted Jesus and earned his admiration for her strength of faith, we learn that *faith* always delights Jesus but that *boldness* may also evoke delight (Mt 15:21-28). From the story of the judge and the widow called importunate, the widow who returns again and again "demanding her rights over her opponent," we discover that *persistence* is an appropriate trait to bring to prayer and that Jesus encourages us "not to lose heart." From this story we also learn that if the "who I am" expects instant results, prayer may be disappointing (Lk. 18:1-8).

From the story of Zacchaeus, a tax collector, "small of stature," we learn that Jesus expects us *to hurry forward with hospitality* for him. "A wealthy man," Zacchaeus was praised by Jesus when Zacchaeus said, "I give half my belongings, Lord, to the poor. If I have defrauded anyone in the least, I pay him back fourfold." From this we learn that if we come to prayer with evidence of *economic generosity to those in need* rather than economic stinginess, the welcome we receive will be commensurately generous (Lk. 19:1-10).

On the other hand, from the mother of the sons of Zebedee (Mt. 20:20-23) who comes to Jesus with the request that her sons sit one on Jesus' right hand and one on his left in his kingdom, the insight comes that *what we ask for may have a cost* we don't anticipate, for Jesus, in replying to her request, says, "You do not know what you are asking." He then suggests that drinking of the cup from which he will drink (persecution) is what it means to be close to him. Elevation to special seats in the kingdom is the prerogative of the Father; to be with Jesus means to serve.

The woman with the hemorrhage (Lk 8:43-48) teaches us that *if we come in deep faith and with need* so great that it is necessarily wordless, the power will come to us from Jesus even if we catch him unawares and even if we hear nothing from him as we are healed. From the leper who begged to be made whole, we learn that *Jesus deeply desires wholeness* for us. In order to lift us up to where he desires us to be, he will touch us wherever we need to be touched no matter how shameful that place may seem to us (Lk 5:12-16).

Over and over we see Jesus as caring and close to those who, in one way or another, reveal their true needs, whether that be a need to be made whole or a need to lessen expectations. If we own our capacity to love and to reveal ourselves when we come to prayer, Jesus may shape that capacity into a deeper trust that sets us free from our fears and resentments, qualities that we by ourselves are incapable of conquering.

When the woman at Bethany poured her love onto Jesus in the form of costly ointment (Mt 26:6-13), the disciples complained. Jesus' response was love in the form of affirmation and gratitude. The woman's free and expressive act of caring, Jesus saw as ministry in the present moment which he enabled to be for a future moment. He then asked his followers to remember her whenever his story was told.

Some of us seek God only when pain is our companion. And Scripture surely encourages us to seek God when we are in pain. But the One who teaches us in Scripture says that it is no weakness to come to the Lord with the ointment of affection. If we listen to Jesus in the gospel and rid ourselves of the moralizing that was the disciples' stance, we may discover a *mutuality of affection* that, remembered, becomes ministering ointment for those days when we feel fit only for burial. John Shea says the following about this kind of good yet unexpected experience: ". . . you relish it, you go with it, you respond to it. You play it out. And you might want to store it away, too. There is a hoarding instinct in prayer experiences. You are a hoarder of good experiences. . . . You might want to stack an experience in your memory and bring it back. I think that is legitimate. We do that with liturgy."[2]

Confusion, fear, annoyance about the way Jesus intended to do the scene was often the stance of the original disciples. It is important for us to remember that before these men and women were sent to face a variety of challenges, they had sustained a time of intimacy with Jesus, feeling his love, witnessing his healing power and his empowerment of those considered less equal or outcast in his society. Learning to trust did not happen overnight. It vanished when Jesus appeared to be vanquished. To be sustained it required the sustenance of the Spririt. Then mission beyond Israel was initiated.

When men and women sense that they will not be sent to tackle the tasks of mission before they are ready to be sent, anxiety about God's demands diminishes. Becoming alert to the concern of God for them, they discover the concerns of Jesus and eventually desire to have these as their own.

The way Jesus responded to persons provides other clues for us on who we are invited to be in prayer. Searching through the gospels for texts relevant to prayer (not limited certainly to texts *about* prayer), we discover that Jesus particularly affirmed listening to the word of God and keeping it. And how can we keep the word of God if we don't know it?

In looking at Scripture we note accounts in which Jesus responds with anger. He scorned hypocrisy. He discerned between God's law and the rules imposed by religious leaders. And he apparently felt free at times about letting others sense his scorn. Even the disciples, whom Jesus cherished, in some instances felt this. "Get behind me, Satan!" was his reply to Peter when the latter attempted to deflect Jesus from his mission. To attack the destiny of Jesus, to try to force him to be other than who he is, received anger as reward. How can we claim to know Jesus if we don't know him as he is in Scripture?

From the story of the publican and the Pharisee we learn that coming to prayer in order to convince God of our self-importance by comparing ourselves favorably to others is one of the least acceptable dispositions to bring to prayer. But this ploy, also used by Martha in the Martha/Mary story, offers insight about who we might be when we come to prayer. The need to cut down others in prayer to earn approval for oneself may indicate hardness of heart but it can also be a sign of insecurity.

"I'm tired! I'm angry! I need help, Master!" Had Martha come in her realness, with her own needs revealed rather than hidden, the response from Jesus may have been different, for those who found ready response from Jesus were those who, in simplicity and honesty, revealed their own needs. Jesus would not be cajoled into making judgments between brothers or about the best seats in the kingdom or into making new wine for old wineskins, but to those who had the humility to reveal their hearts and hurts openly, his empathy was as instantaneous as was his hand extended in healing.

The one I am called to be in prayer is the *real me,* the one whose needs reveal to God my humanness, thereby letting God be God, and freeing me to be the human person God created me to be.

Does What I Pray About Make a Difference?

What I bring to God may be influenced by what has already been discussed. For example, I may shape the content of my prayer according to how welcoming I perceive God to be.

Nowhere in Scripture is there a list limiting the particularities regarding content in prayer. The psalms are evocative of the rest of the Bible, and what we find in them is a variety of content packaged with all kinds of feeling. The desire to know God is matched by the desire to have the Lord know me. Joy pervades some content, agony pervades other. Job, beaten down by every imaginable woe, complains, "Who can get a hearing from you, God? I have said it all from A to Z." Moments later Job proclaims that, in coming before God, he will reveal all that he, Job, has done and "hold my head high in his presence."

Prayer emerges in Scripture from concrete situations; it is addressed to Yahweh out a faith stance that believed that God was dynamically alive and actively concerned. In the Jewish religion, prayer always centers on a *particularity* of life, i.e., an event or a person. To pray for generalities risks offending God by breaking the second commandment. Generality as the content of prayer can trivialize God's name which must not be taken in vain.

In Scripture there is no centering prayer, no searching for the golden glow experience. Prayer in Scripture is not tepid; the content is not skewed by "canned shoulds." The prophets may rage, but it is always heartfelt, and the response expected and received is heartfelt. When the psalmists prayed for the destruction of their enemy, their prayer was that God would enact the justice that was God's prerogative. The psalmists could not conceive of God being other than God.

In light of all this it is unfortunate to discover in our day and age how frequently we folks get into a rut in prayer. Round and round and round we sometimes go, fixated on the same few issues and anxieties. "Take It to Jesus," the name of a gospel hymn, is good advice, but as lay ministers there may be times when we need to take habitual issues to people skilled in listening, counselors or spiritual directors who can help us get to the root of our fixation in order to get ourselves out of our rut.

Faith, World and Feeling

One reason why the content of prayer becomes narrow is because that is who we become. Contemplation aids our escape from this rut because contemplation usually has as its reference point what is beyond ourselves. Becoming more deeply aware of our faith stance is another means for broadening the content of our prayer. Criticism of the Pharisees emerges in the New Testament because they seemed to substitute prayer, ritual and legalism for faith.

To leave the world on the doorstep when one enters the process of prayer invites the charge of "Jesus-and-me" piety. Noticing the world and one's attitudes toward it is being *like* Jesus who looked at Jerusalem; often he didn't like what he saw but rather than looking away from what offended him, he wept, shouted, prayed over it—then went into it. Everytime we dare look at the world as it is in its raw reality and dare to bring this reality to prayer, we live our faith stance and begin its conversion from a belief system to a life system.

Life's content, in its immediacy, does not ordinarily just roll over us. We respond to it with feelings whether we express them or not. Indeed, implying a separation between content and feeling does not reflect reality. Feeling, as well as events and other persons, *is the content* of our lives.

In the gospel accounts we notice that Jesus had the particular gift of being able to be intimate in the midst of a crowd. The ease with which he was able to know his feelings and to express them seems tied to his ability to be intimate. If we attempt to envision Jesus in just one short section in Mark's gospel (5:21—6:56) we see him startled, annoyed, firm, rejected, then amazed, directive, pitying the people, inspirational, and responsive to those in need. Jesus did not seem to be afraid of his feelings. This stance we are invited to have as our stance, even in prayer, if we are followers of his.

What difference does it make in our prayer if feelings are part of the content we bring to God?

To close this chapter on what difference it makes, I will share a story that reveals how feelings make a difference.

After graduation from college in California, one of our daughters came home to live with us and to work in a local firm. One day, about six months after her return, she announced that she had decided to go back to California and seek work there. My husband and I offered the usual reasons parents offer to persuade offspring to stay for a year or two in what seemed to us to be a satisfactory position, but to no avail. Not only was she determined to cross the country, she also intended to depart before Christmas. My remarks about this timetable were numerous and negative.

In prayer, however, my content was all concern and petition. "Dear Lord, please take care of her. Help her find a job. Jesus, please be with her so she won't be lonely on the holidays. Help her to find a job and friends who will love her."

Each time I prayed I left the prayer feeling more anxious than when I initiated the prayer.

Christmas week, as others in the family began to feel uplifted, my feelings descended. One night very late, when I couldn't sleep I left my bed, went into the living room, and lit the Christmas tree. Intending to read the nativity story, I couldn't find the Bible. Discouraged, I began to speak my usual petitions for our daughter.

Suddenly, anger erupted within me. "She's ruining our Christmas, Lord! How could she be so selfish! She belongs home, and I'm *furious* because she isn't here and because it's obvious she doesn't *want* to be here. Why did *you* let her go?"

Letting go of the need to be rational, I let my heart reveal itself to God until the anger spent itself. Gradually, the hurt beneath the anger broke open and began to flow with more than a few tears. She didn't want to be home "for keeps"—that hurt more than not wanting to be home for Christmas.

God did not console. He enabled my sorrow to emerge where anger had been hidden. Then and only then—when God had helped me reveal the truth of myself to myself—did I move toward an acceptance of the truth of things: our daughter was no longer a child-person. I knew that when she left for college in California, I knew that during her stay in California, but I forgot it in the pleasure of having her home again with us. I had, on her return, reverted to a mothering that is the proverbial "closing the barn door"—and done it years after she was well into the process of becoming an adult person, free to search for wholeness in her own way, by her own timetable.

On Christmas she called to tell us of her love for us. Her call was solace, the answer to prayer, the healing for sorrow.

From this experience I was taught once again not to separate my whole self from what I may want, in my worst moments, to perceive as my "holy" self. In going to prayer I'm going to God, the One who sees a holy self *only* in the whole truth of the real self.

Just as crucial is not separating our faith from the reality of who God is. In the chapters that immediately follow, we shall look at Scripture, our source for discovering much about who God is for our tradition.

4

IN THE OLD TESTAMENT YAHWEH MINISTERS

On the Road

When we turn to the gospels, we notice that Jesus' followers met him on the road, that is when they were about the business of living their ordinary lives. He came to them there where these gospel men and women were pursuing their vocations of fishing and tax collecting and mothering and going to the well for water. As a parent, and as a parent who has often held down a secular job while parenting, the fact that Jesus ministered to men and women like you and me while they were on the road of their everyday lives is consoling yet challenging, for his salt of the earth ministry inquires about my salt of the earth ministry toward those whom I meet on the road while I'm hurrying to work or cooking supper for a family that bursts into the kitchen wanting to be heard more than wanting to be fed!

When people on the road met John the Baptist, he pointed them toward Jesus. When people on the road met Jesus, he pointed them to the One he called Father, Abba. In the stories that Jesus told about Abba we find more on the road discoveries. In the parable of the prodigal son, the father rushes down the road impelled by a heart eager to embrace his returning son. Complacency is not a character in this story. The father does not wait for the son to arrive at the estate; his joy is such that he cannot wait.

Jesus also tells us that Abba is the shepherd who searches out hidden places, byways as well as highways, to find one who has lost the way and the road.

Jesus also tells us that Abba is the woman about the everyday task of sweeping in her home. She is in an ordinary setting but motivated by a mission—finding what is not apparent immediately to the eye.

Ultimately our goal in ministry, whatever that ministry is, is to draw people, not to ourselves as individuals, but to community and God. This will be our mission, I feel, only if we are persons who have let ourselves be drawn into a community of discipleship and into intimacy with God, the One who searches for us on the paths we travel day in and day out.

Providence and Ministry

Although we may not articulate it explicitly in words, whether we are advocates for justice, visitors to hospital patients, ministers to engaged couples, lectors or parish council members, our call is to point beyond ourselves to the One able to minister in ways even beyond our dreams. Because of this, a priority for ministerial spirituality is familiarity with ways in which God ministers.

In recent years the parable Jesus told about the prodigal son has sometimes been referred to as the parable of the merciful father. The ministry of the One Jesus called Abba resembled the care of a shepherd, the search of a woman, the generosity of a loving father. It was typical of Jesus to pattern his ministry on the ministry of the One to whom he drew the attention of others, for we find him searching in the streets, we find him with sinners, and we find him near the down-and-outers.

Scripture and prayer may have been his school for this ministry. Through Scripture we, too, can contemplate Yahweh through the manifestations of ministry found in the Old Testament.

A framework of considering God as ministerial is found in Christian tradition. In contemplating God, believers for centuries have affirmed creation, providence, and destiny as entities that are at the heart of his working in relation to the world. Throughout the ages, Christians have believed that God is purposeful:

God created the world;
God exercises providence over it;
God draws it to a final destiny.

In other words, God follows on the act of creating by providing for the world—providence—and by desiring a future for what has been created—destiny. Acknowledging creation is sometimes easier for believers than understanding God's providence. The latter, not yet fully accomplished and interacting with the freedom of humankind, is variously interpreted. Nonetheless Christian believers have often relied on Scripture for clues to God's providence.

What I suggest is that providence, the sustaining of creation and the drawing it to fulfill its destiny, is *God's on-going mission and ministry*. The ministry in which each one of us participates is a part of providence and of destiny, a part of God's providing for the world and of his desires for its future.

With this in mind we are ready to reflect on our ministerial God—on stories of Yahweh in the Old Testament, on accounts of Jesus in the New Testament, and on manifestations of the Spirit today. Our reflection on Yahweh will center on Yahweh's ministries of revealing and fidelity and consider the ministries of teaching, healing, hospitality, and nourishing.

God's Ministry of Revealing

Revealing is a word whose meaning goes beyond teaching or telling, and beyond what we mean when we use the word explaining. In our use of language we usually reserve the word *reveal* for situations in which something is disclosed that is ordinarily hidden, whether we speak of a bathing suit that is "too revealing" or of an incident kept covered up "until he finally got around to revealing what was bothering him."

The revealing that God accomplishes in Scripture is nuanced in a similar way: what was hidden is disclosed, what was expected comes to pass in a way not anticipated, what was ordinary turns out to be extraordinary.

Take the story of Moses, for example. Moses is about the everyday business of tending sheep when he notices that an ordinary bush is not behaving in an ordinary way (Ex 3:1-20). Fire has erupted from the middle of the bush. Climbing the hill with his father-in-law's sheep, Moses may have felt tired, bored, but suddenly he is startled. He becomes curious about the reason for this phenomenon which he calls "strange." His willingness to investigate leads to an even more strange happening—he is addressed by the bush.

Moses replies with the words used by his ancestor Abraham and used by those, like Samuel, who came after him, "Here I am."

In response, the revelations from Yahweh come tumbling toward him, one after the other:

Directions—"Come no nearer," "Take off your shoes."

Disclosure of identity—"This is holy ground," "I am the God of Abraham, the God of Isaac, the God of Jacob." "I Am Who Am."

Historical knowledge—"I have seen the miserable state of my people in Egypt."

Promise—"I mean to deliver them . . . to bring them out of that land to a land rich and broad, a land where milk and honey flow."

Message—"You are to say, 'The God of your fathers . . . has sent me to you and said to me . . . I have resolved to bring you up out of Egypt.'"

By revealing a variety of elements, Yahweh ministers to Moses and to the people of Israel through Moses. To sense the import of this ministry, however, we need to examine the content of the revelation. I Am Who Am is not telling an "oft-told" tale. By giving directions, disclosing identity, showing an understanding of the historical situation of the Israelites, offering a promise related to that reality, commissioning Moses to accomplish a task, expecting that a particular and startling message of deliverance will be handed on by the one willing to say "Here I am," an awesome and vital *newness* breaks into what for Moses started out as an ordinary day.

In other manifestations of Yahweh's ministry of revelation in Old Testament stories, we find a similar pattern. To Abraham and to Hagar, God revealed a promise, to Samuel an unexpected commissioning and a message, to Jacob an identity.

The settings, both human and geographical, where God ministers through revelation in the Old Testament stories, vary as do the feelings of those who receive this ministry, yet surprise is always apparent. Sarah, beyond the age for childbearing, laughs when told she is to be "with child." Abraham, within two revelations from God, is terrified. Birds of prey swoop down on an altar he has built; he "falls into a deep sleep and terror seized him."

Jacob, on the last leg of a long journey, stopping on the bank of a river, resists a stranger by wrestling with him. Later Jacob acknowledges who the stranger is: "I have seen God face to face." Hagar had run away from the ill-treatment of a mistress when God appeared to her by a spring in the wilderness. While Jacob begged his opponent, "Tell me your name," Hagar "gave a name to Yahweh" who had spoken to her: "You are El Roi (God of Vision)."

Lay ministers often take delight in Samuel's story. Three times Samuel said, "Here I am" not realizing that it was God, not Eli the priest, who called. Hannah, Samuel's mother, "speaking from the depth of (her) grief and resentment," was thought by Eli the priest to be drunk when she spoke to God who heard her and responded through the birth of Samuel, a long-wanted child Hannah offered to God in thanksgiving. Tradition reveals Hannah singing a paen of praise, crediting Yahweh for raising

> the poor from the dust, the needy from the dunghill
> to give them a place with princes and to assign them a seat
> of honor;
> for to Yahweh the props of the earth belong,
> on these he has poised the world.
> He safeguards the steps of the faithful . . . (1 Sam 2:8-9).

In the Old Testament we notice what came to be called providence safeguarding the steps of the faithful Israelites, but we also notice that God, at times, startles these faithful by revealing what seems awesome or wondrous or expansively generous: an identity, promises of destiny and progeny, deliverance from oppression.

God reveals what he wants to reveal; the chosen are those whom God chooses. The ministering person who perceives and appreciates this deepens his or her understanding of ministry.

Reflecting on Yahweh's ministry of revelation in a heartfelt way can become a revelation in itself when it leads to the discovery that our God is a personal God, not a distant, mute or proud diety who disdains what has been created. By ministering to us through revelation, God seems to want us to know something about our identity, to know that he is aware of our personal and historical condition, that he is the One who makes promises. Lastly, the ministry of revelation helps us to know what comprises the message for the people God calls his own,

Lectors and religious educators, in their ministries, are entrusted with revelation. (To be authentic, all revealing insights since Gospel times must cohere in spirit with revelation in Scripture.) All ministers as well as lectors and teachers who realize the ordinariness of some of the settings where God has been disclosed, and the variety of persons whom God has chosen as recipients of revelation—from a slave girl to a shepherd—may help others to approach everyday life and the word of God with expectancy and hope.

The Ministry of Fidelity

In like manner, lay ministers of every persuasion benefit from an understanding of the role of fidelity in the Old Testament.

Revelation, for the most part, is one-sided: God does the revealing; Israel and her people reveal what God wants revealed. In the story of fidelity, the traffic goes both ways. God's fidelity is celebrated in the Old Testament, and the fidelity of the men and women of Israel is stressed.

Lay ministers, aware of the images, metaphors, and stories of fidelity in the Old Testament, can engender hope in believers who have, in a singular way, imprinted on their hearts Old Testament images of an angry Yahweh. When we perceive the anthropomorphic images of wrath less as literal manifestations and more as signs of how seriously God considers fidelity by responding to Israel's infidelity, we may become intrigued rather than intimidated by many of the Old Testament stories.

The covenant formed a partnership between God and the chosen people who came to be the nation of Israel. But the part-

nership is not a partnership between equals. A number of Old
Testament stories teach this lesson. Because the dynamic of revelation in this regard is developmental, the context is a living
dialogue between God and the people God has chosen.

Promise, election (being the chosen people), covenant, and
law, all initiated by God, are particular themes of the stories in
the Pentateuch. Because of the favors God has bestowed, infidelity is a great offense whether the individual or the whole people commit this offense against their Creator and covenant
partner.

Infidelity

Rejection of God's ministry of fidelity can happen several
different ways. Through the stories of the golden calf, the stories
of Deborah and Gideon, the story of Job, we will look at three
of these ways:

(1) Turning away for a god of one's own making;
(2) Turning away to turn to the gods of others;
(3) Turning away when suffering comes.

The Golden Calf

The dramatic image of the golden calf occurs in the Book
of Exodus (32:1-6) when the people, impatient because Moses
was taking so long on the mountain top, asked Aaron to "make
us a god to go at the head of us." Melting down golden earrings,
Aaron makes an effigy of a calf which the people worship, crying,
"Here is your God, Israel."

Calling the people headstrong, Yahweh, in a sense, disowns
them by referring to them as "your" people to Moses. Remark-
ing on how short-lived their fidelity was, Yahweh exclaims,
"They have been quick to leave the way I marked out for them
. . ." (Ex 32:8).

In response to Moses' request for forgiveness for the people,
God instead proposes punishing them. Were God's eyes to
glance away from this flagrant instance of infidelity, he would
not be just. Mocking the ministry of God by turning away from

him abuses the bond created by the covenant, necessitating repentance.

Deborah and Gideon

Turning away *to turn to the gods of others* is a more frequent theme in the Old Testament, evoking, again, the crisis of idolatry. As John Dominic Crossan puts it, "The core of Israel's covenant obligations, based on Yahweh's gratuitous deliverance of them from Egypt, was fidelity to himself; all other stipulations depended on this first commandment."[1] The infidelity of the people evokes oppression; when the Israelites had settled down, tribes like the Caananites encroached not only on their territory but on their religious sensibilities, tempting them to worship Baal. The ministry of the charismatic judge is to vindicate this injustice to God.

Blame for the existence of tribes and nations that evoke the temptation of idolatry is interpreted in Old Testament tradition as Yahweh's penalty for the repeated strayings of God's people and as a present test of their fidelity. Yahweh established judges to nurture that fidelity, for Yahweh was with the judge, with Deborah, for example, as she sat beneath the palm tree, interpreting the will of God when disputes emerged.

The judgments handed down were not always appreciated on face value, however. For example, when Deborah tells Barak that she will put in his power a leader of the enemy if Barak attacks, Barak is ambivalent. Afraid because he lacks Deborah's wisdom, Barak urges Deborah to come with him.

In response, Deborah reminds Barak who will get credit for the victory: "I will go with you then, but the way you are going about it, the glory will not be yours; for Yahweh will deliver Sisera into the hands of a woman" (Jgs 4:9).

Indeed, in the retelling of the story of the battle in song, Yahweh's power is celebrated: "The mountains melted before Yahweh, before Yahweh, the God of Israel"; Yahweh's people are celebrated: "Then Israel marched down to the gates; Yahweh's people, like heroes, marched down to fight for him"; and *the faithful one,* Yahweh's judge and leader is celebrated:

Dead, dead were Israel's villages until you rose up,
O Deborah, you rose up, a mother in Israel (Jgs 5:7).

After forty years of peace and prosperity, infidelity emerged
again and the Midianites attacked and stripped the Israelites of
their produce and animals.

The story that follows the story of Deborah is the story of
Gideon and illustrates the dynamic and living quality of the dialogue between Yahweh and one chosen to exemplify fidelity in
a particular way. As mentioned earlier the setting for such dialogue is often ordinary. Gideon is at work, threshing wheat
inside the winepress, when he is told, "Yahweh is with you, val-
iant warrior!"

Gideon is not cowed by this presence; indeed, he sounds as
if he has been waiting for an opportunity to say a few things
himself, for he replies, "Forgive me, my lord, but if Yahweh is
with us, then why is all this happening to us now? And where
are all the wonders our ancestors tell us when they say, 'Did not
Yahweh bring us out of Egypt?' But now Yahweh has deserted
us; he has abandoned us to Midian" (Jgs 6:11-13). To the real
God Gideon brought the reality about the people and himself
that he perceived. Fidelity does not discourage honesty.

Job

Why be faithful to God if he isn't going to return the favor?
This mystifying and perplexing question, at the heart of the
meaning of fidelity, is the challenge of the Book of Job. Job does
not qualify for just punishment for turning away to construct a
god of his own making. Nor did Job turn away to turn to a god
of others. Though the people may be headstrong, Job is steadfast, but the kind of patience he made famous was not an offering to God for his favors bestowed on Job. All matter of misfortune befell Job; he loses oxen, donkeys, sheep, camels, servants,
shepherds, the house of his eldest son, sons and daughters,
before being struck down "with malignant ulcers from the sole
of his foot to the top of his head."

Job's wife, mocking his fidelity to God, urges him to "curse
God, and die." Three friends come, and they are so saddened by

the sight he makes that they rend their garments and sit with him in silence for a week. Finally Job breaks the silence by cursing the day he was born:

Why did I not die newborn,
      not perish as I left the womb?
Why were there two knees to receive me,
      two breasts for me to suck? (Jb 3:11-12).

According to R.A.F. MacKenzie, S.J., Job's three friends are "eloquent defenders of the 'traditional' case . . . Their doctrine is positive, it is sound and helpful . . . contains much moral and religious truth, but they spoil it by exaggeration. They are not willing to leave a margin of uncertainty, to admit limits to their understanding. . . . All the workings of divine providence must be clear to them, explicit, mathematical. . . . (They) forget that (they) are dealing with mystery."[2]

Job accuses them of being dishonest: "Whatever you know I know too." But Job is less concerned with dialogue with them as with dialogue with God:

But my words are intended for Shaddai (The Almighty);
I mean to remonstrate with God.

Telling his friends that silence is the "only wisdom that becomes you," Job asks them:

Will you plead God's defense with prevarication,
his case in terms that ring false? . . .
Can he be duped as men are duped? . . .
Does his majesty not affright you,
dread of him not fall on you?

Job is not content with a "sociable" relationship with God as his friends seem to be, friends who soft-pedal reality, who gloss over paradox in order to come out on God's side. "Job is groping for a more intimate and permanent relationship, based, not on the mere exchange of gifts or services, but on a communion of love."[3] He knows that there are mysteries and marvels beyond human understanding, but not beyond God's power and understanding; he is willing to struggle truthfully with God about paradox and not "explain it away." On the other hand, Job's weakness is to overvalue and argue about his innocence, his not deserving punishment, as if he felt *God were denying it*.

When Yahweh reveals himself, he chastizes Job's friends:

> I burn with anger against you . . . for not speaking truthfully
>   about me as my servant Job has done (Jb 42:7).

In face of the majesty and mystery of God, Job admits that he obscured Yahweh's designs with "empty-headed words" after Yahweh points out that Job, too, was seeking consolation in certainty more than faith.

"Has God's critic thought up an answer?" As searching and questioning was Job's stance, the dialogical flavor of questioning infuses all that Yahweh reveals to Job, at the same time showing the gap between God's powers and Job's, and culminating with the heart of the matter:

> Do you really want . . .
> to put me in the wrong
> to put yourself in the right? (Jb 40:2).

The book of Job asks the anguishing questions of existence and of relationship with a God of power. Through it Job gives the jarring witness to fidelity the saints and martyrs give when we sense that in spite of any suffering, or perhaps because of the visitation that suffering has bestowed on them, their desire is not to turn away (to curse God and die) but to probe more and more deeply into God's heart with boldness and the truth as they see it. The patience Job made famous is far from the passivity we sometimes take it to be. His ministry to others is to reveal fidelity to God.

Other Figures of Fidelity

Understanding how infidelity was perceived in the Old Testament is the groundwork for appreciating the images, metaphors, and stories of the ministry of fidelity.

From Noah to Isaiah

The first allusion to fidelity through covenant in the Bible is in the story of the flood. Because Noah was just and walked with God, he, his family, and two of each kind of animal gathered by Noah are saved. When the flood waters recede, and the dove returns to the ark with the new olive branch in its beak, the sign is given that travail is over. For the poet James Dickey, God's fidelity is symbolized by wings:

> We must put our faith in wings, for after these forty days and nights we know that God has tested us and that God is with us. Wings are what we rely on and they are coming.[4]

Dickey includes the animals when he has Noah say, "We are going to live and bear our children . . ." for in the Bible the first covenant God makes to indicate his fidelity covers all creation:

> I establish my covenant with you and with your descendants after you; also with every living creature to be found with you . . . everything that lives on the earth . . . (Gen 9:3-11).

To signify this fidelity Yahweh shows the rainbow, "a sign of the covenant between me and the earth" (Gen 9:12).

(I can't help but feel saddened by the number of instances when "stewardship," i.e., "men owning the earth," has taken precedence over the partnership God originally established with the whole earth and *all* of its creatures.)

The theology of fidelity, the dominant theme of the Book of Genesis and the Book of Exodus, is exemplified in two other covenants, both more limited in scope than the covenant with Noah:

(1) The covenant with Abraham, extended to his descendants, and signified by circumcision;

(2) The covenant with Israel through Moses, restricted to a people, and signified by sabbath observances.

From Genesis to Hosea the Old Testament unfolds with story after story, image after image highlighting fidelity. In

Isaiah marriage and maternal imagery predominate ("Your creator will be your husband") (54:5). Addressing his spouse, Yahweh proclaims:

> I am now as I was in the days of Noah
>   when I swore that Noah's waters
>   should never flood the world again.
> So now I swear concerning my anger with you
>   and the threats I made against you:
> For the mountains may depart,
>   the hills be shaken,
> But my love for you will never leave you
>   and my covenant of peace with you will never be shaken,
>   says Yahweh who takes pity on you (Is 54:9-10).

The fidelity of Yahweh is revealed in stories of the people from Exodus to Isaiah and in the frequent remembrance that Yahweh is with the anawin—the poor, the helpless, the downtrodden. Fidelity is also exemplified by the stories of Judith and Esther.

Judith

> . . . you are the God of the humble, the help of the oppressed, the support of the weak, the refuge of the forsaken, the savior of the despairing (Jdt 9:16).

Compared to Babylon and its King Nebuchadnezzar, Israel was so paltry and weak that Holofernes, Nebuchadnezzar's military leader, sought informants to learn some things about the Jews. Who could defeat such a powerful leader? Not an army but a woman of faith—Judith.

Judith is a figure evocative of fidelity on three levels: by her own deep piety and wisdom, by her witness to the Jewish elders, and by her loyal action in defeating a rival of Israel and enemy of the God of Israel.

Though wealthy, Judith's preference was for a life dedicated to prayer and charity.

Though not invited, Judith takes a desperate situation into her own hands, summons the elders, and dresses them down for their lack of faith in God when they decide to surrender the town to Holofernes. Telling them they were wrong to defy God, Judith asks:

> Who are you to put God to the test today ... to set yourselves above him? ... You do not understand anything, and never will. ... For God is not to be coerced ... to be cajoled (Jdt 8:11-17).

After telling the elders that she intends an action she will not reveal, Judith prays fervently to Yahweh:

> Give me a beguiling tongue to wound and kill those who have formed such cruel designs against your covenant ... (Jdt 9:13).

Judith proves her faith. Using all her talents and God-given beauty she traps Holofernes in his passions. When she has him "in the palm of her hand," Judith beheads him, saving her people and God's honor, and teaching Israel that the one God chooses as an agent of salvation is his choice, not theirs.

Esther

Judith's story is the tale of a foreign power invading territory belonging to Israel; Esther's story is the tale of Jews as foreigners in another land.

The Persian empire, divided into thirteen districts and one hundred and twenty-seven provinces, was immense. Esther, not revealing that she is Jewish, a counsel that her uncle Mordecai suggests, is chosen by the king to be his wife. Haman, second in command within the empire, orders the extermination of the Jews, testing Esther's fidelity to her people and her God. She begs God: "Reveal yourself in the time of our distress" (Est 4:17).

But her prayer follows her decision, for she has told Mordecai that she must speak for her people: "If I perish, I perish." This "unconditional deliverance of one's whole being to God's discretionary disposition"[5] is the essence of true fidelity. Having made fidelity to Yahweh the priority of her life, Esther takes the risk and reveals to the king, in Haman's presence, that a "persecutor" intends to kill all the Jews: "We are doomed, I and my people, to destruction, slaughter and annihilation" (Est 7:4).

"Where is the schemer of such an outrage?" asks the king, ordering the gallows built by Haman for the condemned Mordecai to be used to hang Haman, the one who condemned.

Esther, the faithful one celebrated in the feast of Purim, who was hesitant at first to reveal that she was a Jew, became "the unpromising instrument that God likes to employ for the dramatic accomplishment of his purposes."[6]

Yahweh's Ministries of Teaching, Healing, Hospitality, and Nourishing

The paradigm for God's fidelity to the people of Israel is the covenant, and the ministries of teaching, healing, hospitality, and nourishing can only be considered in light of the covenant which embodies the law. For example, Yahweh, by establishing the covenant honors the people who became Israel with a generosity of hospitality unique in the known world. *What Yahweh teaches* through the religious institutions of Israel, and through the prophets, *is the law.* Learning the law is nourishment for the spirit as well as the mind, and obeying the law is the sign of fidelity made by the people of Israel. To succumb to false gods, to forget the law and surrender the teaching, is to desert Yahweh. In light of this, what we consider healing today in the Old Testament perception is always spoken of in terms of *the people* returning to Yahweh after coming under the sway of a foreign ruler and succumbing in some way to the lure of a false god. Healing and repentance or return are closely identified, for to throw off the yoke of a foreign oppressor to return to Yahweh and wholehearted obedience to the law often brought peace and prosperity.

Prophets

To obey the law, the law had to be known, making teaching an important ministry in early Israel. Education happened in three ways:

1. Institutionally, through the priests associated with the temple. (In Israel, the priesthood was inherited by families.)
2. Professionally, through the counsel offered by the wise ones and the rabbis in the synagogues. (The rabbi was not ordained. His primary role was that of teacher.)
3. Spontaneously, through the charismatic promptings of the prophets.

Though their functions were distinct, i.e., the priesthood was involved with ritual sacrifice at the temple, each group participated in teaching and worked toward a common objective.

The prophets are difficult to sum up. I discovered that once when working with children. Each child was to choose a type of believer that he or she wished to be. To explain saints, martyrs, apostles, etc. presented no problem. Prophets did. In exasperation, I finally told the children that prophets were "loud-mouths." As soon as I said it, the smallest and quietest child in the group, sighed and said, "Oh, that's what I'd love to be!"

Though putting in a nutshell the ministry of a prophet is well-nigh impossible, no consideration of ministry in the Old Testament is complete unless the prophetic is included. Prophecy was felt to be the way Yahweh chose to speak directly with his people. The ministry of prophets like Jeremiah, Miriam, Isaiah, Amos, and Ezekiel was to reveal the mind of God. Because the prophets were convinced that the realities that forms like rituals *signify* always take priority over the forms themselves, the prophets condemned forms when they felt they had ceased being signs of the reality of God and God's intentions. The prophet was a *public* figure, one considered to have true contact with Yahweh, one who speaks for Yahweh, interprets for Yahweh, one who, consequently, became the *conscience* for the collective entity called Israel. Prophets had a unique vocation from Yahweh; the evidence they presented for this was the testimony of their experience of Yahweh present now in their lives.

Strongly individualistic, the prophets assumed their authority from the confidence evoked by having intense and intimate experiences of Yahweh.

Old Testament scholars generally divide prophecy into three stages:

1. Early prophecy (end of time of Judges and early monarchy).
2. Classical prophecy.
3. Post-exilic prophecy.

The setting for the religious experience of the early prophets was often music and dance. Groups of prophets banded together for mutual prayer, as in this stage "prophetic guilds" were popular. "The ecstatic experience transformed the prophet"[7]—i.e., the prophet Micah felt that he received "the Spirit of Yahweh"; Ezekiel spoke of being "seized by the spirit" and "seized by the hand of Yahweh."

Emerging during the Classical Prophesy period, the professional prophet did not necessarily receive a spiritual call from Yahweh. As prophets were often court officials as well, the charge of "false prophet" became more common. (The prophet could be touched by the Spirit yet still prophesy falsely.)

During this period prophets began to use additional designations for themselves: "messenger of Yahweh," "servant of God," "guardians," "watchmen."

What enhanced the individualistic approach of the prophets was the belief that their "separate personalities were as many diverse instruments through which the word of the Lord was given,"[8] evoking a personalism to the prophetic word not found in the law.

After the exile, as Israel settled and prospered, a hopeful and positive view of the future of Israel prevailed. With the "temple and Torah" offering a stability that endured, the idea of Judaism being a *religion* as well as a people took hold with a concomitant stress on each member's adherence to a rule of life. Prophecy came to be considered a gift of all the people bonded by covenant to Yahweh.

The dynamic of the teaching ministry in prophecy was always *existential*. The responsibility of the priests was the law preserved in the sanctuary, with the high priest considered the principal mediator between Yahweh and the Jews. Prophetic teaching was consistent with the law, yet related to immediate realities. And the prophet, like the figures of fidelity mentioned earlier, was open to facing the consequences of loyalty to God experienced personally as well as collectively, for in the prophet's view "Israel had not been chosen for Israel's sake but for God's.[9] Although "the law and worship (in the temple particularly) were Israel's unbreakable link with her past,"[10] to *judge* the temple was considered part of the prophet's ministry of conscience, and few eminent prophetic figures hesitated about fulfilling that call.

"Repent!" is a word that is not always welcome. For the prophet, whose vocation was teaching and preaching repentance, "suffering is the inevitable fate."[11] There was a difference, however, between "the fate forced on a prophet" and the "voluntary atoning suffering of the *ebed Yahweh*,"[12] the suffering servant of God preached by Isaiah (42:1-4; 49:1-7; 50:4-11; 52:13—53:12) who through suffering "takes the place of the many who should suffer instead of him ... who *reestablishes the covenant.*"[13] (Although many in Israel thought that Jesus was a prophet, in the gospel accounts and, therefore, in the earliest communities, the identity of ebed Yahweh, the suffering servant of God whose sufferings are redemptive, seemed to have been considered more appropriate than prophet. Familiarity with both models and their ministries is helpful to understanding Jesus and ministry.)

The Wise Ones

During the post-exilic time, wisdom became a significant part of the teaching ministry in Israel. Not originating in Israel, the roots of the wisdom movement come from Egypt where it evolved as a means for training young men for court. The contributions from Israel to wisdom movements are a religious dynamism and the inclusion of popular wisdom from the peasant class. The foundations for the wisdom movement in Israel were family and court.

One reason for the emergence of the wisdom ministry was the lack in the Torah of counsel for bringing up young people to practice daily fidelity to Yahweh and the law. That life has the capacity for development may be one of the greatest insights credited to the ministry of the wise ones. From this perspective came a sense that if union with God is achieved in this life, it continues on after death.

The wise one could be a monarch's advisor or an elderly woman who was sagacious. What was common to their ministry was the perspective that *observation of experience*—the environment, the realities of life—led to wisdom. This contemplative ambiance evoked the belief that there are lessons in human experience and that the "divine order is established in things."[14]

That only Yahweh knows the path to wisdom, that only God knows wisdom through and through, was a later development within this ministry. Perceiving wisdom as an attribute of Yahweh's and a characteristic of God's creative activity were other concepts that came to the fore.

These insights help us to see a parallelism between the ministry of the prophets and the ministry of the wise ones. Both stressed a contemplative awareness of ongoing reality; the prophetic minister looked at that reality through the lens of his experience with God and answered that reality with the word received from God; the wise one felt that some manifestations of the divine order could be perceived in the order of existence, but that only God knows the alpha and omega, so only God is truly wise.

The homestead and the historical eventually gave way to include a personification of wisdom, the Spirit of God, ministering directly among the men and women of Israel, revealing the greatness, the goodness, and the generosity of Yahweh.

Revelation, fidelity, and teaching are three significant ministerial strands found in the Old Testament. The prophetic and the wisdom movements braid the three strands together and provide a crucial background for understanding the ministry of Jesus and the ministry of the Holy Spirit.

5

IN THE NEW TESTAMENT JESUS MINISTERS

Two great mysteries are revealed to us in Scripture: our God has befriended us in an ongoing way by actively ministering; our God has befriended us through the gift of the Word, alive and ministering in a fashion that reveals the providential aspects of the Yahweh of the Old Testament. Put more simply, many of the same qualities of ministry attributed to Yahweh in Old Testament stories are found in the New Testament accounts of Jesus.

In the Old Testament narratives phenomena from nature such as the burning bush or significant events—throwing off an oppressor, the birth of a child—become the means through which God ministers; in the New Testament gospels all manifestations of ministry take place in the immediacy of human existential encounter with Jesus. But coherence regarding ministry in Scripture becomes apparent when one notices that the patterns that emerged in Jesus' ministry parallel the patterns ascribed to Yahweh in the Old Testament: hospitality, revelation, nourishing, teaching, healing, and fidelity. The *importance* Jesus placed on ministry was mentioned in Chapter 1 by citing his reply to John the Baptist's messengers when they asked, "Are you the one to come or do we look for another?" In answer, Jesus *identified himself* by sending a report of his *ministry:* "the blind recover their sight, the lame walk, the lepers are made clean, the deaf hear, the dead are raised to life, the poor are hearing the good news—and happy the one who does not find me a stumbling block" (Mt 11:2-6).

Jesus' Ministry of Hospitality

The New Testament begins with welcome as its theme. The instances of hospitality as an initial note in the gospels are striking. In Luke's gospel Elizabeth offers the hospitality of her house to Mary who has rushed into the hill country of Judah after an encounter with Gabriel during which she felt disturbed and perplexed by his revelations. Hospitality of house is quickly followed by hospitality of heart expressed with Elizabeth's cry, "Of all women you are most blessed." Elizabeth tells Mary of the honor and joy she feels because Mary has come to visit; then she repeats the theme of blessedness: "Yes, blessed is she who believed that the promise made to her by the Lord would be fulfilled."

The affirmation inherent in Elizabeth's hospitality seems to seize Mary's heart, healing any distress evoked by Gabriel's revelations and moving her from an interior acceptance ("I am the handmaiden of the Lord") to an interior acclamation of the greatness of God. Mary responds to Elizabeth's hospitable greeting with the exultation of the Magnificat: "The Almighty has done great things for me!"

A second element—newness—is revealed in this passage, indicated by the fact that the first human communal religious experience of Luke's gospel, initiated by the presence of the Holy Spirit, takes place between two women (Lk 1:39-56).

In John's gospel hospitality breaks in immediately. The first words of Jesus in John are: "What are you looking for?"—in some versions, "What do you want?"

In Matthew's gospel, after the temptation and the call of the disciples, Jesus is immediately hospitable to those who are "suffering from diseases and painful complaints of one kind or another, the possessed, epileptics, the paralyzed" (Mt 4:24). In Mark's and Luke's gospels, Jesus initiates his public ministry by welcoming one whom others avoid—a demoniac—whom he cures.

Jesus exercised his ministry of hospitality to the point of causing scandal. To those whom his official religious culture had made outcasts, like lepers, and women during times of menstrual flow of blood, Jesus offered the hospitality, not only of his heart but of his hand. This hospitality of touch was significant, for his religious culture had for over a millennium made touching those in a permanent or temporary outcast situation a taboo (Lk 5:12-16; Mk 5:25-35).

To welcome outcasts is a true test of hospitality. The healing of the woman with the issue of blood (Lk 8:43-48; Mt 9:20-22) is particularly significant here, for this appears to be a rare instance where a person was able to draw the power of healing from Jesus without his awareness or intention, indicating how available to others Jesus was.

The woman in this passage, fearful of touching Jesus because of the taboo, fingered only "the fringe of his cloak," yet the hemorrhage stopped. Jesus then knew he had been touched, for he said, "Somebody touched me. I felt that power had gone out of me."

The extent of Jesus' ministry of hospitality shocked his disciples. They try to stop a man healing in Jesus' name "because he is not one of us," but Jesus is even hospitable to ministry done in his name without the sanction of being in his immediate group.

Since Vatican II, the ministry of hospitality has been newly appreciated by the church. In local communities, ushers and greeters have come to perceive, not only the importance of their ministry, but also the import of the way in which they exercise their hospitality, the sensitivity toward others that is the foundation for this ministry. This forms a bond with the ministry of evangelization. Hospitality is the hallmark for one who is called to evangelize, and evangelization can be a fruit of the ministry of hospitality extended by the usher.

How much the church has changed in regard to hospitality was illustrated for me at a parish workshop when the keynote speaker said that in the past he had always thought of ushers as "bouncers," i.e., those who keep out or throw out rather than those who invite in.

Ecumenical hospitality is another fruit of Vatican II. While joint worship is hardly commonplace, joint efforts for peace and justice and for marriage ceremonies are characteristic in a number of settings. Opening the door to ecumenism exemplifies the greater openness to the world emergent in the church with the onset of Vatican II. (Perhaps the time has come for us, as church, to exercise more fervently the ministry of hospitality to others within our own denomination, particularly toward the laity. For example, when my oldest daughter was in college, we moved to a city one hundred miles away from where she had lived as an adolescent. When she decided to marry, our new parish setting had little meaning for her. Officially she could marry her Catholic fiancé nowhere else. "It's too bad he isn't a Protestant or a Jew; it would be so much easier" was the message relayed to me by more than one priest.)

Jesus knew how to be hospitable to those in his *own* culture, including children, and he ministered first to the house of Israel, particularly to the poor, ill, and otherwise needy and, as noted earlier, to those neglected or oppressed by the official ministry of his tradition, lepers and women. Although faithful to the people of his own tradition, Jesus extended hospitality to others beyond his tradition, even to designating them as symbols with religious significance. For example, there were tensions between Jews and Samaritans. Jesus reconciles this by referring to a good Samaritan as the model for how the good Jew should love a neighbor. Servants and shepherds were looked down upon by society in general. Jesus used shepherd to refer to himself, i.e., John's passage on the good shepherd (Jn 10:1-21). There are also frequent identifications of leadership with servanthood (Mk 10:41-52).

One of the most radical expressions of Jesus' ministry of hospitality, and one not suggested in Scripture prior to Jesus, is his urging his followers to imitate God's compassion by loving their enemies (Lk 6:27-38; Mt 5:43-48). An equally striking passage that exemplifies Jesus' ministry of hospitality is the designation by Jesus of those in a crowd around him as his true relatives, claiming them as intimate to himself as mother and brother, and sending that message back to his mother and brothers who arrive and want to see him. For us today that may be perceived as only a gracious sentiment expressed to strangers. One has to understand that, in the tradition of Jesus, belonging to the tradition totally depended on blood relationship. It is not that converts were not welcomed so much as there was no theological mechanism for their entrance into the tradition since the promise given to Abraham that his descendants by blood relationship were to be the people of God's covenant. When Jesus, "looking round at those sitting in a circle about him,"says, "Here are my mother and my brothers. Anyone who does the will of God, that person is my brother and sister and mother," a new identity erupted in religious tradition (Lk 8:19-21; Mk 3:31-35; Mt 12:46-50).

"Anyone who does the will of God"—that "anyone" might be a good Samaritan or a good centurion. Paul perceives this when he says that there is in Christ Jesus "neither Jew nor Greek, man or woman, slave or free."

Identifying the ministry of hospitality with ushers and evangelizers surely does not exhaust the potential for this ministry. Hospitality, if we are followers of Jesus, is the foundation for all ministries within the church. Hospitality is called to be the sign of the church in society and a sign of relationship within the church, whether the ministry that evokes it is accomplished in chancery office or confessional, soup kitchen, parish council or advocacy hearing. Being hospitable to one another's perceptions, ideas, and life experience as well as sharing sacrament at liturgy and refreshment at coffee hour and church supper is what it means to follow Jesus in the way in which he ministered to the men, women, and children he encountered on the streets, in the hills, and by the shores of Galilee.

Jesus' Ministry of Nourishment

How God nourished us by sending Jesus among us is particularly meaningful to me because nourishing has been a significant part of my life as a mother.

Putting bread on the table, and spaghetti and meat loaf and chocolate pudding and salad (and doing it before 6:30, if possible, which is seldom possible because I don't get home from work till 6:00) is a lot of what my life has been about, along with fixing trays for sick children and baskets for picnic suppers.

Nourishing has many dimensions. Two of our daughters, as young children, ran high fevers. Nourishing then meant sitting by bedsides, sometimes in fear and frustration, trying to coax sips of water or juice down hot and hurting throats. As our daughters grew in age and grace, nourishing minds, hearts, and spirits took on added importance.

All of that may be why I savor the way Jesus nourished: he fed the crowds. He fed the people, one by one.

Jesus fed Bartimaeus, not by telling him what he needed, but by asking him what he wanted. Jesus fed the woman at the well by telling her everything she ever did. By showing her to herself, he became for her the living water that enabled her to consider him as the Messiah he acknowledged himself to be (Jn 4:1-30). In another setting, as a guest at supper, Jesus fed the woman who scandalized Simon the Pharisee by washing Jesus' feet with her tears, her kisses, and her ointment. She was nourished by Jesus' affirmation of her gift of loving and the worth of herself. And Jesus might have fed Simon, who was about the business of feeding Jesus, when Jesus pointed out that abundance of love and forgiveness of sin are related (Lk 7:36-50).

In the Lukan accounts, Jesus never seemed to tire of revealing the superabundance of God's creation and providential kingdom. Whether pointing to the beauty of the lilies of the field (Lk 12:27-32) or the dragnet overflowing with the fish (Lk 5:1-11) or telling parables of mercy and invitation to strangers along the highways and byways, Jesus reminded his hearers that God cannot be outdone in the sharing of table and in the hospitality of heart.

The profusion of images of banquet and feast in the New Testament takes the meaningful moments of ordinary life—meals—deepens them to the level of profundity and lifts them up to the heights of celestial celebration. Ordinary loaves and fishes, picnic style, become a miracle (Mt 14:13-21); bread broken and shared becomes Presence that is recognized as death risen to new life (Lk 24:35); the promise that his followers will partake of the heavenly banquet with Jesus (Mt 26:29) precedes his sharing his body and blood with them and then for them and all humankind as the two closely related titles for Jesus—Lamb of God (paschal lamb) and ebed Yahweh (suffering servant of God) indicate.

Jesus is the nourishment of the One he called Abba, given to all peoples for all earthly time.

The seasons of the liturgy and the sacraments of the church, particularly the Eucharist, keep this alive in our memory as nourishment for faith. Liturgical planners and lay ministers of the Eucharist may have a special awareness of this. The variety of ways Jesus offered nourishment, however, indicates that this ministry is pertinent to many ministries in the church today. The food of praise given to the centurion is an example for those engaged in the ministry of evangelization. His transformation of the wine at the wedding at Cana encourages those helping couples prepare for the transformation that marriage is. The story of Dives and Lazarus and the Beatitudes, by revealing how close to the kingdom are the suffering and the poor, inspire believers committed to social justice ministry.

"Give us this day our bread for the morrow." This early variation of the Lord's Prayer referred to the need for nourishment that would strengthen body, heart, and spirit for the challenge of facing the expected apocalyptic end-time. "Give us this day our bread for the morrow" is an appropriate rendition of the Our Father for us who live in an age that faces the famine of life that a nuclear holocaust could wreck. That the peace of the Lord found at the table of Jesus will become God's kingdom and will done on earth is a petition that all ministers may want to make their own.

The Ministry of Jesus as Teacher

The settings of the mount, the synagogue and the temple are the backdrops for perceiving Jesus in the formal role of teacher. The number of times he is addressed as rabbi indicates an association between Jesus and teaching. Although religious education has roots that stretch far back in the history of Judaism, other ministries, accomplished sensitively, need no formal setting to be part of the tradition that educates about the graciousness of God. Character and quality, not time and setting, tell the tale. The formal settings for teaching found in the gospel may enable us to perceive more easily the frequency with which Jesus engaged in this ministry through encounters on the road and in response to questions about topics as diverse as what should one do to inherit eternal life and what does one do about taxes and Caesar. The teaching of Jesus about life mirrors and incarnates the teaching of Yahweh about law.

Some, like the rich young ruler, turned away from the lesson this rabbi imparted. That Jesus' counsel was a lesson is imaginatively shown by a New England poet, Mary Kennedy, in her play based on this incident and used in the Vineyard Community for a rite of reconciliation. In the play, the rich young ruler turns away initially. As the lesson sinks in, he sells all he has except a marvelous cloak which he wears as he searches once more for Jesus whom he finds being taken down from a cross. Repenting his delay at responding to the teacher's wisdom, he finally parts from his cloak by wrapping the body of Jesus with it.

That the lessons we impart as lay ministers don't always "sink in" at first is sometimes our own fault. If we flaunt expertise rather than share wisdom, if we substitute advice-giving for teaching, we don't minister as Jesus did. On the other hand, we may present a teaching, as Jesus did, that goes beyond what is normative for our religious culture and society. This kind of lesson needs time to "sink in," and educators need to give time and space for that process to happen before rushing ahead with the next lesson on their own agenda but not necessarily on the agenda of the gospel.

The Healing Ministry of Jesus

In the Old Testament there seem to be far fewer individual manifestations of healing than in the New Testament. But a parallel can be found regarding healing. The Old Testament prophets proclaim again and again that the only way the people of Israel can be healed is by a return to God. And closeness to God as restorative is at the heart of what Jesus meant the many times he said, "Your faith has healed you."

Jesus presents a model in his healing ministry, one that can deepen our sensitivities. The ease with which Jesus let credit directed toward him slip by provides an example for all ministers who hope that healing will be the fruit of their ministry. In the healing ministry, we merely facilitate the faith within the persons we encounter and the transforming power of God.

Closeness to God is what heals, not ministers. That bears repeating: Closeness to God is what heals, not ministers.

Jesus' Ministry of Fidelity

> ... Jesus Christ, the faithful witness, the first-born Son, who
> was raised from death and who is also the ruler of the kings
> of the world ... (Rev 1:5).

> This is the message from the Amen, the faithful and true wit-
> ness who is the origin of all that God created (Rev 3:14).

The epistles of the New Testament as well as the Book of
Revelation, based on the vision of John, celebrate the fidelity of
Jesus. In the gospel accounts of Jesus' life we find the ministry
of fidelity lived out in his prayer, his preaching, and his passion.

1. Prayer

The custom of the Jewish people in the time of Jesus was to
offer three hours of prayer each day. Because this pattern seems
to have continued into the life of the earliest Christian communities, and because Jesus frequently urged prayer as an
expression of fidelity to God, it is safe to conclude that three
hours of prayer was Jesus' style as well.

"From the heart" and "in the midst" also seem to charac-
terize Jesus in prayer. The pressures of crowds or the persistence
of skepticism did not prevent Jesus from lifting his heart up to
the Father. In spite of the skepticism of others, at the tomb
where Lazarus was interred, Jesus thanked the Father for hearing his prayer (Jn 11:41), and then called Lazarus to come out
from the darkness of death. In Jerusalem, when the crowd inter-
rupted his petition that the name of God be glorified (Jn 12:29,
33), and when the disciples crowded around him exultant at the
success of their ministry (Lk 10:17-22), Jesus was not deflected
from his ministry of giving blessings and praise to Abba. Jesus
prays for Simon, and his prayer is that Simon Peter have faith
that does not fail (Lk 22:31-34). That certain healings could be
accomplished by prayer alone, Jesus pointed out to his followers
(Mk 9:29).

Though Jesus often followed his own Jewish tradition in
regard to prayer, he also innovated. This creative freedom is best

seen in two unique elements that were part of the spiritual life of Jesus. First, Jesus seemed to be drawn to spending long periods, often at night, in solitary prayer (Mk 1:35; 6:30; Mt 14:23). Second, as mentioned earlier, it was Jesus' custom to refer consistently to Yahweh as Father, a title rarely used in Hebrew Scripture, and to address the Father in prayer as Abba, an endearment never used in Jewish prayer. Jesus' use of Abba (dearest father) tells us that his fidelity had as its source *relational intimacy with God,* providing for us appropriate example for our spiritual life if we follow Jesus and model our ministry on his way and wisdom.

Fidelity to both God and prayer frequent the content of the teaching and preaching of Jesus. Pretentiousness in prayer is to be avoided by his followers, for the Father, already knowing the heart of the faithful one, desires only honesty, humility, simple sincerity and a forgiving spirit. What we are looking for, what we desire, we are to bring to the Father in prayer, alone or with others, without ceasing. Faith by itself can move mountains (Mt 17:20); faith with prayer can evoke the presence of Jesus (Mt 18:19-20).

2. Preaching

Jesus seemed able to sustain fidelity to God with loving fidelity to the people. The kingdom about which he preached tirelessly was a kingdom open to all who, in loyalty to God, cherish it and move forward in its ascetical but abundant spirit. Fidelity is as important in the New Testament as in the Old Testament. In the more ancient Scriptures, the fidelity of the entire people of Israel is the frequent refrain; in the New Testament, fidelity of the person (faith) is often the focus. A person's fidelity will find reward:

> If you have faith, everything you ask for in prayer you will receive (Mt 21:22).

> Everyone who has left houses, brothers, sisters, father, mother, children or land for the sake of my name will be

repaid a hundred times over, and also inherit eternal life (Mt 20:29).

Happy that servant if his master's arrival finds him at employment. I tell you truly, he will place over him every-thing he owns (Lk 12:43-44).

Come, you whom my Father has blessed, take for your her-itage the kingdom prepared for you since the foundation of the world (Mt 25:34).

Fidelity to God and reverence for the need of the people to pray seemed to motivate Jesus to the action that was his final challenge to the leaders of the religious establishment of his times—the expulsion of the dealers from the temple. Jesus' voice, rising above the clamor of pigeons, money-changers, and turning tables, proclaims: "Does not Scripture say, 'My house will be called a house of prayer for all peoples? But you have turned it into a robbers' den" (Mk 11:17).

3. Passion

If intimacy with God is a sign of fidelity, and abundance its promise, cost is a condition. The good shepherd lays down his or her life for the sheep; there is no greater expression of love; there is no way to be more faithful. At Gethsemane Jesus prays that there be another way. His will is ready to obey, but his heart and spirit anguish with what the ministry of fidelity, taken to its ultimacy, means for his own life.

In the passion, the ministry of Jesus' fidelity merges with the mystery of his mission. Stripped and suffering, he accom-plishes both. The cross becomes the fruit-bearing prayer: never heard before—never, in its particular uniqueness, spoken by another since—a word never silent—a word never fully comprehended.

Jesus' ministry of fidelity is our redemption, a transforma-tion that unites us in oneness with God, with community, and with humankind.

Jesus' Ministry of Revealing

In our consideration of the ministry of revealing in the Old Testament several elements were noted: what is hidden is disclosed, the expected comes to pass in a way not anticipated, the ordinary turns out to be extraordinary. Comparable instances of the ministry of revealing are so numerous in gospel accounts of Jesus' ministry that examples must suffice.

As mentioned earlier, Yahweh, in the story of the burning bush, did not tell an "oft-told tale," and Jesus, the "sign of contradiction," similarly demonstrated in gospel stories a "newness" that startled the neighbors in his hometown (Lk 4:16-30), the Pharisees and priests in his culture (Mt 12), the disciples (Mk 10:35-40), and those who witnessed his healings (Mk 7:35). Over and over the evangelists tell us that the crowds Jesus encountered on the road marvel at his works.

Parallel to Jesus' ministry of revealing are the manifestations of revealing noted in the discussion of the burning bush— giving directions, making a promise, and commissioning, as well as disclosures of identity, knowledge of historical situation, need for deliverance, and message.

In the formation for discipleship outlined in chapter ten in the gospels of Luke and Matthew, the evangelists show Jesus offering a number of *directives* to his followers—from the practical: "Shake the dust off your feet" when the peace you extend is not accepted, to the profound: "Beware of men" because they will "hand you over to the Sanhedrin and scourge you in their synagogues." But anxiety about defending oneself is not to be the stance of the disciple, for when the disciple speaks, the Spirit will speak in that disciple.

The religious and ethical framework of the times seem to be *the historical situation* of concern to Jesus, for this is where his prophetic ministry of revealing has its focus. Matthew signifies this in his account of admonishing Jerusalem—

Jerusalem, Jerusalem, you that kill the prophets and stone those who are sent to you! . . . Your house will be left desolate . . . (Mt 23:37-38).

And in Mark we have the example referred to earlier of Jesus expelling the dealers from the temple:

> Does not scripture say: "My house will be called a house of prayer for all the peoples?" But you have turned it into a robbers' den (Mk 11:15-19).

About the relevance of history Jesus is prophetic:

> Alas for you, Chorazin! Alas for you Bethsaida! For if the miracles done in you had been done in Tyre and Sidon, they would have repented long ago, sitting in sackcloth and ashes (Lk 10:13-15).

As in the Old Testament, *deliverance* is linked to the broader historical context, and Jesus' revealing in this regard is related by the evangelists in apocalyptic terms. In the Lukan account, prior to the passion, for example, Jesus is presented as describing the historical situation of the future:

> For great misery will descend on the land and wrath on this people. They will fall by the edge of the sword and be led captive to every pagan country, and Jerusalem will be trampled down by the pagans until the age of the pagans is completely over (Lk 21:24).

> When these things begin to take place, stand erect, hold your heads high, because your liberation is near at hand (Lk 21:28).

The *promise* implied here is apocalyptic deliverance, interpreted as the "end-time" being at hand. (Yet, to disciples Jesus also promises "the hundredfold," in this life, as well as in the hereafter.)

Jesus goes beyond his circle of disciples in revealing promise, and the sign of that promise is heavenly celebration (when, searching for mercy, the sinner turns to God; when the stray is found by the shepherd; when the good thief joins Jesus in death; when an enemy is loved). God is our model for love of enemy as well as for love of neighbor, being the One, Jesus reveals in Luke, who is kind to the ungrateful and to the wicked (Lk 6:35).

In the Old Testament Yahweh often *commissioned* those to whom he revealed himself to go to the people of Israel, and in the New Testament we have several examples of Jesus sending the disciples (Lk 10:1; Mt 10:1; Jn 20:17, 21). On occasion Jesus sent those whom he healed, such as the Gerosene demoniac.

The last elements concerning Jesus' ministry of revealing that parallel what we have seen in the Old Testament are revelations of *identity* and *message*. Jesus was not predictable about directly revealing his own identity as Messiah as we have seen in his response to the question from John the Baptist. John's gospel suggests that he told the woman at the well in Samaria that he was the Messiah. But he asked his followers who others claimed him to be.

When, on inquiry, Peter indicated that Jesus was the Christ, Jesus credited the Father for the revelation, yet rejoiced at Peter's cooperation in the process. As Cullman points out, "From a very early date Christians were accustomed to connect the designation. 'Christ' with the name of Jesus. Jesus-Christ meant Jesus-Messiah. . . . The designation even gave the new faith its name. Its followers were called Christians (Messianites) for the first time in Antioch (Acts 11:26)."[1]

The *newness* Jesus revealed concerning the *identity of Yahweh* is shown, as previously mentioned, by his addressing the Father intimately as "Abba." And the message he revealed was intimately tied to his Abba—where there is God there is kingdom, plenitude of growth and feast and payment for those who recognize the kingdom's value by being ready for its coming whether that be future or today, hereafter or in their midst. Being ready for its coming was crucial if they were believers; if they are not ready they will be replaced by those who may not know of its existence but who will not spurn the invitation for entrance. Jesus spoke so often of God in the context of kingdom that the birthing of a new identity between God and peoples emerged: where there is God, there is room for peoples (kingdom of heaven), and where there are peoples, let there be room for God (kingdom on earth).

In the last chapter, when we considered the burning bush, I noted that once Moses had responded to this manifestation of God's presence, "the revelations came, tumbling one after the other." We have just considered the rich flow of revelation engendered by Jesus. In the Old Testament there seems to be a good deal of other data—narrative, song, recounting of history—between more direct revelation (I say more direct revelation because all of Scripture is revelation as the Word of God). While having all the variety found in the Old Testament, Jesus' ministry of revelation evokes an even greater intensity through its frequency, fullness, and fruitfulness—e.g., it is not only Jesus whose ministry causes the people to marvel; his seventy-two disciples return rejoicing and he marvels at what God has brought about through their ministry.

Before his public ministry, direct revelation is something that happens most frequently when a person is in solitude (Abraham, Moses, Ezekiel, Mary). With Jesus, revelation itself, there is such a spilling over of things being revealed that a method, the parable, seems to have been adopted to protect the sense that revelation will continue to be disclosure of what is hidden and not immediately comprehended by all (if its meaning were immediately apparent it would hardly be revelation).

The affinities between Yahweh and Jesus are enhanced, not diminished, when we see the ministries of Yahweh brought to completion in Jesus who thrust them forward into mission that is ongoing through the ages, part of God's providential love, and part of the forward movement of the destiny which God, through the Holy Spirit, is calling humankind.

No one of us can imitate the ministry of Yahweh or the ministry of Jesus. All of us, banded together in community, image Paul's sublime concept—the body of Christ who now ministers to the world in the mission initiated by Jesus.

To be *imago Dei* means that each of us, as well as our church in community, can express hospitality, nourish, teach, and heal. Because of who God is, the revelation of God is unique. Because of who Jesus is, the fidelity of Jesus is unique. Nonetheless, through one's ministry and one's life *each of us is called to reveal* that our God is a God of compassionate love and saving power, and to reveal that fidelity to Jesus through prayer, proclamation, and passion, is at the heart of faith and sustains ministry.

The earliest men and women who ministered in Jesus' name did so through the gift of resurrection faith. In other words, all that they did, they did impelled by the experience of death turned to life, of Jesus risen among them. T. W. Manson points out further significances between the risen Jesus and ministry, showing that in the public ministry, the model is Jesus "leading the way and the disciples following on behind, sometimes with courage and confidence, sometimes in perplexity and apprehension, but still following."[2] The Easter event "tells them that the leadership they have known and learned to rely on continues and will continue."[3]

"The second point is that this continuing leadership is leadership in a continuing Ministry. The Risen Lord, as it were, picks up the threads of his work,"[4] teaching along the road to Emmaus, urging Peter to feed his sheep, nourishing his followers at meal time.

"The third point which emerges from the study of the Resurrection narratives is that Jesus continues to delegate his work to others. . . . One of the most impressive features of the Resurrection narratives is that they show the Risen Lord doing the same thing" he had done earlier: " 'he would send them out' to do the kind of work that he himself was doing, in his way and in his spirit."[5]

In conclusion, Manson states: "The Resurrection means above all just this, that Christians do not inherit their task from Christ, they share it with him. We are not the successors of Jesus, but his companions. That is the measure both of our privilege and our responsibility."

6

IN THE FAITHFUL THE HOLY SPIRIT MINISTERS

In perhaps the most poignant moment of the film *Tender Mercies,* Robert Duvall, a faded country folk singer, tells the daughter from whom he is estranged that he doesn't remember a hymn she claims he sang to her as a child. When she leaves the house, Duvall turns to the window, and in its diffused light quietly sings the hymn about Jesus going down to the waters to be baptized "in the usual way" and God blessing his Son by sending his love on the "wings of a dove."

We are touched by his sadness because he cannot be open to the intimacy his daughter craved and indirectly invited, but we also, too easily perhaps, identify with the way Duvall shies away from what might bond them into something inseparable. Intimacy with others scares some of us; intimacy with God alarms some of us. The Church can provide all the means available in this world for encouraging intimacy with God, but the Church can't *make* it happen. The ingredients necessary for that are two: the Holy Spirit and an open welcome within the believer's heart. In the words of St. Basil the Great: "Through the Spirit we become intimate with God."

St. Basil's voice is the first of many we will hear in this chapter, a chapter with more quotations than all the rest of the chapters combined. This may be jarring because we are not prepared for the multitude of voices we will hear. But that is key to the ministry of the Holy Spirit. First, that we are seldom prepared for it. And, second, that the earliest believers in Jesus were not prepared for the multitude of voices and tongues that broke out at Pentecost and jarred the men and women of Jerusalem. To hear the Holy Spirit in our tradition and in our church today, we have to listen to the voice of more than one, or more than a few.

For a description of the ministry of the Holy Spirit, St. Basil the Great is an interesting source (ca. 330–379 A.D.). As David Anderson says, according to St. Basil "we can tell who the Spirit *is* by examining what He *does*":

> What does the Spirit do? His works are ineffable in majesty, and innumerable in quantity. . . . If you consider creation, remember that the heavenly powers were established by the Spirit (Ps 32:6). . . . Christ comes, and the Spirit prepares His way. Working of miracles and gifts of healing come from the Holy Spirit. Demons are driven out by the Spirit of God. . . . Through the Spirit of God we become intimate with God. . . . Resurrection from the dead is accomplished by the operation of the Spirit. He gives us risen life, refashioning our souls in the spiritual life. . . . We know that our souls attain such a high degree of exaltation through the Spirit. Understanding all this, how can we be afraid of giving the Spirit too much honor?[1]

Theological Muddles Concerning the Spirit

"Understanding all this, how can we be afraid of giving the Spirit too much honor?" St. Basil asked this question because he was embroiled in a controversy. Prior to the fourth century, theological battles had started over humanity/divinity issues pertinent to Christ, but, according to David Anderson (author of the introduction to the 1980 edition of St. Basil's Treatise), "The question of what sort of being the Holy Spirit was simply had not been answered. . . . St. Basil realized that by writing a book affirming the equality of the Spirit with the Father and the Son, he could make a water-tight case for orthodoxy. . . . His primary objective in this Treatise is to clear up the muddle. . . . "[2]

Doctrinal muddles may be one reason why, according to Yves Congar, the Holy Spirit has been pastorally neglected in the Christian churches of the West. But Congar's claim, "The Holy Spirit has sometimes been forgotten,"[3] is perceived primarily as a displacement. Congar cites the Eucharist, the Pope, and the Virgin Mary as historical "substitutes" for the Spirit.

If the Spirit is overlooked one infers that the *ministry* of the Spirit is less appreciated and less realized than might be expected considering our long standing belief in one God who is Three Personed. Perhaps this lacuna is why Pope John XXIII, in convening the Second Vatican Council, prayed, "Renew in our days your miracles as of a second Pentecost." There are some who would claim that the Spirit readily responded to the request of John XXIII in that a fruit of the Council is an appreciation for the bestowal of the gifts of the Spirit. The emergence of lay ministries and the charismatic movement may be other indications of this.

Since Vatican II, dealing with the simultaneous implementation of so many post-conciliar changes has absorbed our attention; in this turmoil our notice of how much we as a people have come to value the ministry of the Holy Spirit may not yet be apparent. Before Vatican II, however, few lay Catholics appreciated the ministry of the Holy Spirit. Most associated the Holy Spirit with authority; some associated the Holy Spirit with grace, wisdom and/or mystical prayer; few associated the Holy Spirit with community and ministry.

Startling Catholic believers with a multitude of surprises, Scripture, rediscovered in importance following Vatican II, engendered more diverse reflection on the Holy Spirit and more depth in understanding the breadth of the Spirit's influence and empowerment. That the Spirit dwells within the believer, making the believer a temple (1 Cor), that the Spirit lives within the community of believers bestowing gifts on the people for the upbuilding of that community (1 Cor), that the Spirit sends disciples on mission and will speak through the disciple if he or she is challenged (Mt 10; Mk 13; Lk 11), that the love of God is poured into our hearts by the Spirit (Rom 5)—all these *ministries of the Spirit* had the ring of *new revelation* to believers who had seldom heard the *original* revelation. As Pope Leo XIII (1810–1903) said in his encyclical *Divinum Illud:*

> Perchance there are still to be found ... even nowadays, some who, if asked, as were those of old by St. Paul the Apostle, whether they have received the Holy Ghost, might answer in like manner: "We have not so much as heard whether there be a Holy Ghost." At least there are certainly many who are very deficient in their knowledge of Him.

They frequently use His name in their religious practices, but their faith is involved in much darkness.

This darkness of ignorance did not seem as widespread in the early church *where local church communities gave evidence of the presence of the Spirit:*

> I am exceedingly, in fact beyond all measure, cheered as I think of your happy and glorious endowments. So deeply implanted is the gift of the Spirit that has been graciously vouchsafed to you! ... I really witness in your community an outpouring upon you of the Spirit from the wealth of the Lord's fountainhead (The Epistle of Barnabas, ca. 117 to 130),

and *where the gifts given by the Spirit were valued:*

> This same Holy Spirit, that works in those who utter prophecy, we call an outflow from God, flowing out and returning like a ray of the sun Athenagoras (second century).

> Let us make use of those generous gifts and seek to avail ourselves of this most essential boon. ... "We have received the Spirit which comes from God, so that we may know the gifts which have been generously given to us by God" (Hilary of Poitiers, 315–367 A.D.).

> No one could be so uninitiated in the mysteries of the Gospel as to be unaware that a man or woman has but one vehicle that can carry him or her to heaven ... the wings of the descending Dove (St. Gregory of Nyssa, ca. 335–394 A.D.).

The Wings of the Dove

If many in our recent past *were* so uninitiated in the mysteries of the Gospel, poets and mystics have often been the ones in church community to stake faithfully their hopes on the wings of the Dove. And saints, in particular, have been the ones to live wholeheartedly the life and ministry of the Spirit residing within them, often enhancing creatively the Christian community, exemplified by Francis, Teresa of Avila, Ignatius, and Catherine of Siena. As Jurgen Moltmann puts it, "By socializing, the Spirit individualizes; and by individualizing, he socializes."[4]

"Socializing"—A Ministry Exercised by the Spirit

In religious tradition, socialization is belonging to a people (the ancient theme of Judaic-Christian history). In Christian tradition, this "belonging" is engendered by the Holy Spirit. By finding a "new identity in Christ"[5] and a place and way to live this new personal identity within the church and world, the believer contributes both to the community and to the mission of the community in the world. "Socialization and individuation are two sides of one and the same operation in the history of the Spirit."[6] One recent concrete manifestation of this dynamic on the parish level is the experience of adult catechumens in the RCIA program; cradle Catholics, on the other hand, are apt to imbibe socialization and individuation "with their mother's milk" and may not have a *consciousness* of the process that adult catechumens have.

To associate with other believers is part and parcel of what it means to be a Christian. This is the *intent* of the Holy Spirit and is *enabled* by the Spirit.

From that very brief sketch of the socialization side of church and the ministry of the Holy Spirit, we turn to the individuation enabled by the Spirit. (Moltmann's language is helpful as is his model, for, in considering the ministry of the Spirit, one must avoid any either/or—i.e., the Spirit only working in the church as institution or community *or* the Spirit only working in and through an individual.) The ministry and gathering that Jesus initiated emphasized both individuation and socialization, a dynamic continued and deepened and intensified by the Spirit at Pentecost and through the faithful ever since. As Congar states:

> The distinctive aspect of the Spirit is that, while remaining unique and preserving his identity, he is in everyone without causing anyone to lose his originality. This applies to persons, peoples, their culture and their talents. The Spirit also

makes everyone speak of the marvels of God in his own language.[7]

"Individuating and Transforming"—
Ministry Exercised by the Holy Spirit

How then does the Spirit minister within the individual believer?

According to Christian tradition, genuine and extended personal encounter with the Holy Spirit does not efface or diminish personality. It transforms. Karl Adam, who was a convert to Catholicism and a psychiatrist, perceived that "the creative Spirit" enhances the individual personality and fashions "there a faith that, growing intimately and organically out of the individual personality, determines the whole mental and moral outlook of the believer. . . . "[8]

In his classic book, *Varieties of Religious Experience,* William James indicates two kinds of conversions—the dramatic and immediate type, and the more extended dynamic of gradual transformation. This process of individuation within socialization by the Spirit is described by John Shea as personal "re-creation" which involves a "long and arduous process":

> Christian conversion is not a movement from one stage of innocence to another. It is a movement from a struggle wrongly conceived to a struggle rightly conceived . . . for the purpose of transformation.[9]

Part of that process often involves a perception of what Adam sees as the difference between who one is and who one can become. On perceiving this, the believer

> is afraid, trembles, and draws back. But whithersoever he may go, the loving importunity of the Holy Spirit pursues. . . . The new light may pierce him, yet it is constantly giving a new insight into things . . . with ever new yearnings for God and with new impulses towards good. A pitched battle begins between the new love and the old . . . and the conflict is so glorious, that the angels of heaven rejoice to witness it.[10]

Perhaps only a psychiatrist could relish so readily the interior struggle that the ministry of the Spirit evokes. But Adam's description is akin to what St. Ignatius of Loyola suggests by "discernment of spirits." Within the believer, Ignatius perceived spirits engendered by the one he called "the enemy of human nature" and spirits engendered by God. Discerning these spirits and facing the choice of moving with the Holy Spirit or with theenemy of human nature, according to Ignatius, evokes a struggle sometimes characterized by periods of "desolation" and periods of "consolation." Because it is simplistic to identify every feeling of spiritual buoyancy as the work and way of the Holy Spirit and every dark impulse as the work and way of the enemy of human nature, a retreat director or a spiritual director is often a valuable and needed companion for this process of discernment.

Desperately needing "a Love that loves us more than we love ourselves" (Shea), we reach that "vital turning point of the religious life—self-surrender" (James). Shea quotes E. D. Starbuck's insightful commentary on this juncture:

> (The believer) must fall back on the larger Power . . . which has been welling up in his own being, and let it finish in its own way the work it has begun. . . . [11]

The believer is now ready to experience the power of the Spirit given over to a ministry of love. Alfred Delp, S.J. (1907–1945), imprisoned and executed for resisting the Nazi regime, indicates that embracing the Spirit of God in the very center of one's life brings "healing in its roots and source."[12]

The tremendous vitality noticed in those faithful to the struggle that Adam, Shea, and Ignatius describe "come out on the other side" knowing with their hearts an insight described by Karl Barth: "The Holy Spirit is God giving us the freedom we were seeking in vain within ourselves: freedom for God."[13] Shea sees it as "the work of an ironic God who abundantly gives us what we desperately want but not in the way we want it." We lust for achievements; we receive gift, the gift of loving God, ourselves and our neighbor.

Now welcoming and open to all that the ongoing ministry of the Holy Spirit confers, this believer encourages "the Holy Spirit to penetrate and blend with the life impulses, purifying and completing them with its own intensity and assurance" (Delp).[14] This individuation can resonate with the socialization that is church (yet sometimes challenge it) because the Holy Spirit's ministry enables the believer and the community to bear the fruits of the Spirit. Shea calls this "the release of other-centered energies" . . . "the release from chronic egocentricity."

One example of what that looks like is given by Louis Dupre in his book *The Other Dimension* and resembles the "salt of the earth ministry" spoken of in Chapter 1:

> . . . love for the person already *present* which gave birth to the concept of neighbor, that is, *he or she who happens to be there* regardless of personal qualities. Neighborly love climaxes in love for the enemy, the supreme challenge to human affection. It is, as Kierkegaard defines it, the love for the man or woman one encounters rather than for the man or woman one prefers.[15]

The ministry of the Holy Spirit never erases our desires or our capacity to desire; the Holy Spirit helps us to shape our desires. And, according to Ignatius, there can be no greater desire than the desire to be with and like Jesus:

> Whenever the praise and glory of the Divine Majesty would be equally served, in order to imitate and be in reality more like Christ our Lord, I desire and choose poverty with Christ poor, rather than riches; insults with Christ heavy with them, rather than fame; I desire to be accounted as worthless and a fool for Christ, rather than esteemed as wise and prudent in this world.[16]

People easily back away from such a desire, perceiving it as extreme and as something one would have to accomplish on one's own. The latter, of course, is impossible, for to have the desire and to live out the desire are gifts of the Spirit. Until one experiences the transforming process that is the ministry of the Spirit, understanding the meaning and language that Ignatius uses here can be difficult. Unfortunately, phony models—imitation saints done up in artificial flavors or born-again zealots—stimulate in many of us an automatic, negative reflex that evokes fear that our own personal identities would be rubbed out or made bizarre if we surrendered to the process the Spirit invites which is what Vatican II speaks of as "the call to holiness," a call to wholeness that enhances rather than erases our personal identity.

Holiness: The Spirit's Call

On the other hand, to attempt to respond to the call to ministry without responding to the call to spiritual wholeness is folly—for self and for church. Though there have been instances too numerous to record, ministry makes a poor substitute for holiness. Without a response to the Spirit's call to holiness, the believer may lack the empowerment needed for ministry to be other than just a function.

> A soul that is given over to the Holy Spirit no longer walks; she flies.[17]

We need to hear the stories of those who have gone before us; as pilgrims we hunger for them to light our way. As searchers, we may be annoyed yet envy those without ambivalence like Egeria, a pilgrim in the fourth century. With incredible energy and stamina, she embarks on a rigorous journey and single-mindedly visits holy persons, holy places, and holy buildings throughout Palestine, Egypt and Constantinople before returning to her homeland.

Ideal Types

The relevance of holiness is as significant today as it was in the fourth century. We can appropriate the essence of those who lived enabled by the ministry of the Spirit in ages past. Our tradition has a wealth of examples that suggest this.

In *The Analogical Imagination* David Tracy presents *classics* of theological tradition and argues that classics can include *persons.* Lawrence Cunningham, in *The Catholic Heritage* describes some of these classics, calling them ideal types, perceiving Catholic tradition as "a history of people in all their particularities extended in time."[18] To me each type reflects, in its own way, the process that is the ministry of the Spirit described as conversion earlier.

Ideal types that Cunningham portrays include: *martyrs* whose blood, according to Tertullian, was the seed of the church; *ascetics,* particularly those living monastic life which was intended to be exemplary and eschatological; *mystics,* many of whom have been popular with the people of their culture but not with church authorities, and who therefore, in spite of their direct experience of God, have not been cannonized; *theologians; pilgrims; artists* (from creators of icons to Michelangelo to Flannery O'Connor); *saints.*

Now and in the near future, peacemakers and justice advocates may, under the impetus and with the help of the Spirit, swell the ranks of the "ideal type" Cunningham calls "activists."

The Spirit's Ministry Transforms and Empowers the Ordinary and the Extraordinary

Whether tracing the lives of the ideal types that Cunningham poses, or the process of engagement that Adam and Shea describe, or the responsive love that Delp delineates, we see that the ministry of the Holy Spirit is *transforming* and *empowering.* Being open to that process to its fullest extent is the best preparation for ministry.

According to St. Paul, in the earliest church the faithful were the saints, and the saints were the faithful.

In considering *the idea of saint,* we find a perpetual tension between the attraction that the *extraordinary* evokes and the appreciation that fidelity to the *ordinary* evokes. As the latter is so often the dynamic of lay lives, lay persons need to be alert lest it get lost in a media age that seems so frequently to focus on newsmakers. Saints, says Cunningham, often "demonstrate . . . that a new sense of consciousness is entering the church," yet it is crucial to remember that some saints "have lived the fullest possible spiritual life *available* in their own time and place."[19]

The great openness to the Holy Spirit invited by Vatican II may provide a wealth of new opportunities, ministries, and missions that will evoke an age of saints not seen since the fifteenth century. Lay saints, living in fidelity to the ordinary, even if not cannonized will undoubtedly be greatly represented in that number. They will be those who have experienced "a Love that loves us more than we love ourselves," one that in the process enables us to love ourselves and others.

A new age of saints may also emerge from what Cunningham calls the contemporary desert, e.g., "the industrial factory, the Gulag, the Nazi concentration camp, the jails of Latin America, Russia, the Far East."[20] According to Cunningham, these new deserts (and we might add refugee camps and ghettos) provide the setting for "the wrestlings of the new hermits in the desert" who battle, not with beasts as St. Anthony did, but with "jackboots, advanced chemical gases, instruments to shock, mind-altering drugs and bureaucratic regimentation."[21]

The parallel between the lives of the desert fathers in ancient times and today is exemplified by two writings Cunningham cites:

> One of the monks, called Serapion, sold his book of the Gospels and gave the money to those who were hungry, saying: I have sold the book which told me to sell all that I had and give it to the poor (Sayings from the Desert Fathers).

> You want to be,
> excuse me,
> First get free
> of that excess
> of goods
> which cram
> your whole body
> leaving no room
> for you and even less
> for God (Dom Helder Camara, *The Desert Is Fertile).*[22]

Origen (first half of the third century), a brilliant early Christian scholar, felt that the Holy Spirit works *only* in the lives of saints. To us that seems extreme, yet nowhere does the ministry of the

Holy Spirit seem more explicit than in the life of a saint. That life mystifies us, inspires us, defies us, and often irritates us. Such excess! But was not Pentecost excess, with tongues of fire, foreign tongues, gifts bestowed on the many rather than the few, on the ordinary rather than on the extraordinary?

What a sorry church we'd be without the saints!

In Marcy Heidish's fine novel *Miracles* on the life of Elizabeth Seton, we hear the devil's advocate, Fr. Thomas Chandler, say to himself at the end of the story:

> I couldn't then; but now I see the shimmer of this woman in the data. I see her burning through a near-constant fog of loss to me. Perhaps that's what saints do, after all. Perhaps they are not perfect beings, flawless icons. Perhaps they are, instead, lightning rods. Conductors. Conduits. People struck with, fired with, filled with something from beyond themselves: so struck, so fired, so filled, they channel it to others. . . . Her suffering, her searching, her losses somehow fueled it. And by the end, she had the blaze that makes things happen; even extraordinary things. I believe that now.[23]

Naming The Spirit

New images of God, inspired by the "landscape" or the times or the culture and encouraged by the Spirit, are to be expected. The Holy Spirit is more up to date than the rest of us. Or as Moltmann put it:

> . . . the Spirit can be termed the "power of futurity" . . . the beginning (Rom 8:23) and the earnest . . . guarantee (Cor 1:22; 5:5) of the future . . ."[24]

If we identify the Spirit only with the past, only with tradition, only with institution, we invite ourselves to forget that promise of the New Testament come true—that it is the ministry of the Holy Spirit to break through with new creation as happened at Vatican II. In a like manner, we err if we divest the early church of apostles. According to Congar, "The ministry of the Spirit is first and foremost something that has to be carried out by the apostle, who lays the foundation (1 Cor 3:10; Rom 15:20)."

As creative impulse of God, the Spirit vivifies the minister's creativity as well as faith (both essential for ministry) and the faith of the community. Who I am and what I do, who we are and what we do, become one, become unity, through the ministry of the Spirit. Through this the church becomes vivified . . . the pilgrim people march forward.

The titles and names for Jesus are few compared with how the Holy Spirit has been identified throughout the ages. Often our gratitude is owed to poets and mystics who seized the freedom for God that the Holy Spirit confers, who are said to experience God more directly than the rest of us, and who have revealed to the rest of us, not only creative images and names for the Spirit, but also the inventiveness of the Spirit's ministry. Officials and ministers of the church, in documents and preaching, have also named the Spirit in a variety of ways.

Listening to some of these names and titles may help us perceive how *we* name the Spirit in our own prayer and lives.

More than a thousand years ago Bernard of Clairvaux rhapsodized on the Holy Spirit as the kiss of God, while St. Hildegarde perceived the Spirit as "beast-plate of life, girdle of beautiful energy."

"Advocate" (Gospel of John) . . . "Lord and Giver of life" (Nicene Creed) . . . "who spoke in the Law and preached through the prophets, and descended to the Jordan, and spoke through the apostles and lives in the faithful" (Creed of Epiphanius, bishop of Cyprus ca. 374) . . . "the Holy Ghost is called a *gift;* for by the term gift we understand that which is kindly and gratuitously bestowed, no anticipation of remuneration being entertained" (Catechism of the Council of Trent, 1566).

Some use contrast to make more keen our appreciation for the Spirit.

For example, John Dcnne (1573–1631): "Oh holy Ghost, whose Temple I Am, but of mud walls, and condensed dust. " John McMahon referred to the Spirit as "Guest of my soul" and "Friend of all my years" and spoke of the indwelling of the Spirit as more significant than the Blessed Sacrament: " . . . the presence of the Holy Ghost in our souls is still more amazing because God's presence in the Blessed Sacrament will cease on the last day, whereas the presence of the Holy Ghost in our souls will never cease. It will last for all eternity."[25]

"Like a gardener cultivating our souls" . . . "like a dove in her nest" . . . "like a mother leading by the hand her child" (Curé of Ars, 1786–1859); "Teacher of Truth" . . . "Spirit of Christ" . . . "Paraclete" (Pius XII); "the love of God in me" (Carlo Carretto); "pledge of the abiding presence of Jesus" (Dietrich Bonhoeffer).[26]

Some of the above names, roles and images were made public through the official teaching of the church; they may, in known and unknown ways, nourish the faith and ministry of the people of the universal church.

Some of the above names, roles and images were made public by mystics, poets, and saints. Though binding on no one, these may also, in known and unknown ways, nourish the faith and ministry of the people of the universal church.

Some names and images of the Spirit are shared only with a loved one, or a spiritual director, or a local community. These may also, in known and unknown ways, nourish the faith and ministry of others. It is important to listen to our interiors, to hear the stories there, to see the images (often evoked by the Spirit) there, and to let them move into expression—into stories we tell, poems we write, paintings or songs we create. Our history is overflowing with the interior becoming exterior in this way, a way akin to what is generally acknowledged as the effect of the ministry of the Spirit—bearing fruit.

Sometimes the movement is from the exterior to the interior—expressions and sharings of friends nourishing our faith and ministry. Sometimes an exterior image or idea will lie fallow for years, then spring to life. My story of the Spirit runs in that direction.

After my "long and arduous process" of "personal recreation," in gratitude and to sort out by thinking out loud, I wrote a play about the Trinity. Several people read the play and arranged for a production at the Berkshire Theatre Festival's Winter Writer's Workshop.

Ursula Niebuhr, former chair of the religion department at Barnard and widow of the noted Protestant theologian Reinhold

Neibuhr, came. After the performance she said, "The Holy Spirit ought to be a woman."

"Oh, no," I replied. "That would seem bizarre!"

While Mrs. Niebuhr chatted on about Sophia and the Greek tradition, my husband kept asking, "If the Holy Spirit can come as a dove and a flame, why not as a woman? Isn't a woman as good as a dove or a flame?"

Six years later I took the play out again to sort out by thinking out loud. I remembered Mrs. Niebuhr and thoughts of taking the risk to see if she was right. She was. Having the Holy Spirit in the feminine form adds a dynamism impossible to evoke when the Trinity is perceived only in male imagery.

What had happened in between?

I had discovered the Old Testament—more precisely, the wisdom literature mentioned earlier, the Jewish writings that include Job, Proverbs, some Psalms, Ecclesiastes, Sirach, writings developed during the four centuries before Jesus' birth. In this section of Scripture, according to Congar, "Wisdom is brought so close to the Spirit that the two realities are almost identified, at least if they are viewed in their action. . . . This Wisdom comes from God. She is his action for the benefit of his creatures, enabling them to go straight . . . she—or the Spirit— even has a cosmic function . . . holding the universe together. . . ."[27]

In the Book of Wisdom, I was particularly struck by chapter 7:

> In her there is a spirit that is intelligent, holy, unique, manifold, subtle, mobile . . . distinct, invulnerable, loving the good, keen, irresistible, beneficent, humane, steadfast . . . all-powerful, overseeing all. . . . Though she is but one, she can do all things, and while remaining in herself, she renews all things; in every generation she passes into holy souls and makes them friends of God, and prophets. . . . She reaches mightily from one end of the church to the other and she orders all things well. . . .

The influence on me was striking—not so much related to writing the play (I never attempted a production of the revision), but in my spiritual life. Those who were at Pentecost perhaps habitually sensed a flame when the Spirit was mentioned or preached or counseled or met in prayer. Since my experience with the wisdom literature and the play, I always sense woman when the Spirit is mentioned or preached or counseled or met in prayer, and I know that I am valued, am being transformed, am empowered for ministry.

As my husband said, "If the Spirit can come as a dove or a flame, why not as a woman? Isn't a woman as good as a dove or a flame?"

If the spiritual life of the church has been enhanced by contemplative images of the Spirit as the kiss of God, as gift and as gardener, then perhaps we should ponder, as we do the *idea* of saint, the *idea* of the Holy Spirit, of God *not* being revealed in a precise and deliberate form (a complementary idea to the Logos *being* revealed in the precise and deliberate form of Jesus). Having no fixed image affirms the imaginations of those who have encountered forcefully the Spirit interiorly down through the ages. The relevance I see in this for the lay minister is explained by Ann Bedford Ulanov:

> Imagination captures the transformation of the Spirit. From simple images of particular experiences of the Spirit grow the large symbols and visions of religious tradition. We lose connectedness with the tradition and doctrine when we lose touch with even subliminal images in our experience of mystery . . . the novice in the spiritual life must nuture every tiny experience *through imaginative responses to it*. Only then do we find a bridge to the record that religious tradition has made of human experience and the divine.[28]

Muddle and Upheaval

At the beginning of this chapter I quoted David Anderson who spoke of the "muddle" St. Basil tried to clear up regarding the Holy Spirit. That the post-conciliar church is evoking muddles is probably an understatement. And it is not only that the changes themselves, coming all at once, created a muddle, but also that we as a people, whether eager, neutral, or resistant to particular changes, discovered that after the period of novelty a settled-in or back-to-normal situation failed to come to pass. Instead, practical implementation was followed by reflection which led to more question or wonderment or challenge. For example, soon after Vatican II adult education programs emerged and featured courses in Scripture. Lay people flocked to these courses expecting answers. Answers they received—but answers that stimulated more questions, more muddle, more upheaval.

Discerning where the Spirit is in the muddle and upheaval might not have been so difficult had ignorance or famine regarding the Spirit, the fact alluded to by Pope Leo XIII, not been the antecedent of Vatican II.

From famine to feast, some say, rejoicing as they see the Spirit *in* the upheaval, *in* all the movements engendered by Vatican II, reminding us that the first Pentecost caused upheavals and muddles yet a strong sense of the presence of the Spirit of God. Faith, these optimists remind us, that is open to change, not complacency, is the stance the Lord seeks.

Theological muddles and church upheavals are not new; Christianity *was* initiated through muddle and upheaval. If, as yet, we do not perceive with the accuracy we'd like the ministry of the Spirit in our time, we can begin to identify what we *do* perceive as the remarkable probability that is the work of the Spirit.

For many that inventory would begin with the Vatican II Council itself, the hierarchical council that unleashed much of the muddle and upheaval. And it might include the vitality now found with frequency *in the local church, in the sense of community, and in the gifts of the Spirit become ministries* that are celebrated as post-conciliar fruits of the Spirit. (The next chapter will feature a focus on those elements.) Earlier in this chapter we saw that the initial step in *personal* conversion was staying with the struggle. Should we expect the *communal and institutional conversion* process we witness today to happen differently? The call of the Spirit may be to stay with this struggle.

In addition to identifying where we perceive the ministry of the Spirit, we can ask the Spirit to enlighten us about our own personal *stance* toward the muddle and the upheaval. To close this reflection on the ministry of the Holy Spirit, I will contemplate four elements that may prove valuable in discerning one's stance toward the muddle.

Discerning the Spirit

"Lord, I believe; help thou my unbelief." Hope is an essential boon to remedy the kind of unbelief that sometimes is a nearby neighbor to belief. When dying and rising are happening simultaneously, the horizon always appears unsettled. We can pray to understand the plowing and reaping going on simultaneously "in our midst" as part of the "history of the kingdom of God," i.e., "The history of the kingdom of God on earth is nothing other than the history of the uniting of what is separated and the freeing of what is broken. . . . "[29]

Second, we can remember that ministry of the Holy Spirit to which we are called to respond regardless of the day, the year, the place, the upheaval, the muddle: the Spirit's call to holiness. As the devil's advocate in Marcy Heidish's novel about St. Elizabeth Seton says, "I see her burning through a near-constant fog of loss. . . . " Muddle, like fog, obscures the vision; saints are beacons—conduits—through it.

Third, whatever God is revealing within the church in this age will cohere with what God has revealed in Scripture. Often hopes stay vibrant by contemplating the *dynamic* of Yahweh's ministry of revelation found in the Old Testament and that ministry accomplished by Jesus in the New Testament—what has been hidden (the Holy Spirit?) is disclosed; what was expected (life in the church to continue) comes to pass in a way not anticipated; what was ordinary (daily life, prayer, liturgy, laity, women, mission?) turns out to be extraordinary. Disclosure of identity, promise, directions, and deliverance are frequent themes of the ministry of revelation in Scripture; can we expect less from the Spirit of God ministering within us and with us today?

Lastly, in our communities and in our personal life, we can "keep in touch" and "imaginatively respond" to the "simple images of particular experiences of the Spirit" we have. (Each is an experience of God. The Holy Spirit is not a mediator between us and a God who is distant. When we experience the Spirit we experience God.) In the contemporary contemplative tradition, it is Thomas Merton who perhaps has most evocatively imaged the ministry of the Spirit:

> Sophia is the mercy of God in us. She is the tenderness with which the infinitely mysterious power of pardon turns the darkness of our sins into the light of grace. She is the inexhaustible fountain of kindness, and would almost seem to be, in herself, all mercy. So she does in us a greater work than that of Creation: the work of new being in grace, the work of pardon, the work of transformation from brightness to brightness *tamquam a Domini Spiritu.* She is in us the yielding and tender counterpart of the power, justice and creative dynamism of the Father.[30]

When we sense the Spirit ministering to us (uniting who I am and what I do), and to the community of our local church and our universal church, let *us* celebrate with the jubilation that Gertrude von le Fort (1878–1971) proclaims:

> (The Spirit) has come over me
> as buds come on a spray . . .
> . . . has sprung forth in me
> like roses on the hedgegrows.
> I bloom on all my branches
> in the purple of his gifts.
> I bloom with fiery tongues,
> I bloom with flaming fulfillment,
> I bloom out of the Holy Spirit of God.[31]

From heaven, Gertrude von le Fort, I trust, will forgive me if I share her poem one more time, this time with "we" for "I" to celebrate the experience of the Spirit of the last two decades that so many have found Christian community in church to be.

> (The Spirit) has come over us
> as buds come on a spray . . .
> . . . has sprung forth in us
> like roses on the hedgegrows.

We bloom on all our branches
in the purple of the gifts.
We bloom with fiery tongues,
we bloom with flaming fulfillment,
we bloom out of the Holy Spirit of God.

7

DISCERNING BASIC ELEMENTS OF MINISTRY

For, from, and *with* are small words that often do hefty work. In the previous chapters attention was centered on God engaged in ministry and ourselves as we function spiritually. Now it is time for integration. Prepositions will do the hefty work with our assistance on the sidelines.

This reminds me of a "moving day" story.

Some years ago my family moved from New Hampshire to Massachusetts. Early in the morning, the movers arrived and walked from room to room in silence. Finally one said in exasperation, "This is a nine-room bungalow with a cellar and a garage! We were told it was a three-room apartment!"

Two hours later, with four friends drafted to help, the first stick of furniture was transported into the moving van. Fifteen hours later, long after midnight, the furniture, dumped unceremoniously on the first floor of our rented eight-room dwelling, glared at me accusingly. I fled to the one "arranged" room—the master bedroom on the second floor. A week later, the furniture was still the ferocious enemy.

When would I feel up to dealing with all of it?

When would we ever begin to feel "at home" again?

Where to begin to make sense of it all?

A commentator on Vatican II once likened the aftermath of the Council to an incident similar to our move from New Hampshire to Massachusetts—the furniture of our faith was in such disarray that few knew where to find the needed pieces and even fewer knew how to get them arranged in order for us to feel "at home" once again.

Where to begin to make sense of it all?

In our reflections we have started to make sense of the relationship between theology, spirituality and ministry. But what about all those other pieces of furniture related to ministry and spirituality—catechesis (instruction), evangelization, ecclesiology (theology of the church) including community and authority, shared responsibility and so on? When will maps be available to help us arrange this furniture so that we can begin to feel at home?

What is needed is what we have available to us in everyday life to help us remember or retrieve information easily, formulas like a "Thirty Days Hath September" or "i before e except after c" or "the quick brown fox jumped over the lazy dog." In attempting to be a cartographer for the terrain of theology, ecclesiology, Scripture, community and pastoral "horse sense" in regard to ministry and spirituality, I discovered that a key for such a map is the preposition, or rather three common prepositions—*for, from,* and *with.*

There are two ways to use the for–from–with formula to organize our thoughts about ministry. For example, lay ministry is engaged in for God; the call comes from God; the ministry is done with God. For, from, and with the church is a similar pattern.

However, to further a sense of integration, an alternate route will be used. That is, we will look at how ministry is *for* God, *for* the church, and *for* oneself, and follow the same pattern in regard to "from" and "with."

For—What It Means

Purpose gives a sense of meaning to our lives. Restlessness, resentment, and even guilt can emerge when an activity seems to have no purpose or a purpose with which we are at odds. A child doing homework because he or she should do homework in order to pass is doing it *for* a different purpose, and conseqenty with a different attitude, from the child doing homework *for* love of the subject.

There is a world of difference between ministering for God because one feels that his or her ministry *should* be for God—i.e., it's a homework assignment—and ministering for God because one has a personal relationship with God—i.e., love of the subject. Whenever "should" is the motivator of an activity, duty, will, and discipline are the directors behind the scenes. Whenever a personal relationship of love is the motivator of an activity, commitment of the heart is the director behind the scenes, a director who can, on occasion, show will and discipline.

To be *for another* means that one will rally to the defense of the other, will try to please the other when the occasion presents itself, and will often communicate the virtues of the other. It's no wonder that we prefer friends (and God) to be "for" us rather than against us.

The adolescent who has fallen in love can spend endless hours contemplating what will please or displease the beloved. But adults in mature relationships are also sensitive to what "goes down well" with the persons or groups to which their hearts are committed.

To be *for* someone rather than against that person indicates not a passive, vague support, but a range of specific behaviors. If our ministry is for the Lord, the same can be said of it. If in our ministry flows from our discipleship, then we are invited to ponder what Jesus might have meant when he said, "Follow me." "Follow me" is the initial step in being *for Jesus.*

Ministry That Is for the Lord

"Follow me" was the call Jesus made to all types of persons in the crowds that gathered about him. The gospels seem to indicate two particular kinds of response to "follow me"—leaving home to give witness and staying home to witness to one's neighbors.

That two different patterns of following prevailed is substantiated by early church history where we find itinerant preachers who traveled and domestic, settled communities like those at Corinth and Thessalonica.

That Jesus himself, as preached in the earliest communities, indicated that some persons could follow him and be for him by remaining with their families and remaining faithful to their daily tasks sometimes comes as a surprise to believers, but it is a line of evidence that lay persons engaged in voluntary ministry might contemplate.

"Jesus loved Martha and her sister (Mary) and Lazarus," yet he did not seem to call them to be on the road with him. Although Mary Magdalene, when cured of the demons possessing her, followed Jesus by accompanying him on his travels, the man cured of demons in Gerasa did not, in spite of the man's pleas to be with Jesus in this way. Jesus refused his request, saying, "Go home to your people and tell them all that the Lord in his mercy has done for you." At home, in the area of Decapolis, this man became a missionary for the Lord (Mk 5:1–20).

In the gospels we find no ladder effect, implying that those who had the most faith in Jesus were the ones called to travel far and wide with him. In all of Israel Jesus found no one to match the faith of the centurion, but Jesus also respected the choices and responsibilities the centurion had already made (Lk 7:1–10).

The decision on following does not seem to depend on how much Jesus has revealed about himself. To the woman at the well he reveals, for the first time, himself as Christ, the expected Messiah. The woman, proclaiming this to her townspeople, is the first person in the gospels to preach that revelation. The giftedness accompanying this honor, however, is to be lived out in the midst of what is familiar to the woman (Jn 4:1–41).

What trust Jesus reveals in those earliest of believers who ministered in the spirit of his message!

Knowing Jesus is the first and most fundamental lesson for their ministry. In John's gospel, two of John the Baptist's disciples begin to follow Jesus. He turns and asks them what they want.

"Rabbi, where do you live?"

"Come and see," encourages Jesus.

"Come and see" is an invitation extended to all who follow, including those who minister today. By coming to Scripture and seeing Jesus engaged in ministry, we get to know "where he lives." In addition, we discover in his friends, and in those to whom he preached, human qualities that reside in us. Following Jesus on his journey through Scripture, we, in our hearts, encounter him and become more readily *for* him in our lives, including our ministry. We find ourselves rallying to his defense, engaging in action that is pleasing to him, and telling others about his virtues. All this can be accomplished in our hearts and can vivify our lives without our need to leave family and friends and the responsibilities that our ordinary lives demand. Without ever "leaving home," we find ourselves feeling "at home" regardless of how often the furniture of our faith or church is rearranged.

Ministry That Is for The Church

Through the process of knowing Jesus we often find growing within us a desire to be *for the church*. Lay persons, in recent years, for example, have often revealed fidelity to the church by participating in rounds of activity within the church.

Two years ago I led a workshop session on voluntary lay ministry and professional lay ministry. The purpose of the workshop was to clarify differences between the two. On a chalkboard the amount of time spent in church ministry weekly was estimated by each voluntary and each professional minister in the room. All thirty of us were surprised to see that a quarter of the volunteers spent as much time in ministry as paid professionals working full-time.

The tendency for the parish lay person to be involved in multiple voluntary ministries can be enriching for the community. But are there dangers in this kind of commitment of the heart?

Those who answer in the affirmative usually cite:

—the potential for these ministers to be "used" by others in unjust ways;

—the difficulty of applying criteria to those in voluntary service;

—the problem of "letting go" in order to give others an opportunity for ministry.

When I did full-time, voluntary ministry, one marked difference in contrast to my ministry today was quality of time. During my volunteer days, life at home was like Grand Central

Station—projects spread across the dining room table, the phone ringing off the hook, supper rushed so that I could dash off to a meeting.

My ministerial studies forced me to look squarely at how my whole life would be for God and how my service would be for the church. One fruit of this was the determination to be fully present to my family at meals and during the evenings when I was at home. Discouraging phone calls during those times was the first, but not the easiest, step to take. As a married deacon once said to me, "I get exhausted just thinking about how to begin to make home less a three-ring circus than it is because of my ministry."

In order to be *for the church,* is this kind of dedication necessary?

Or does this kind of dedication sound the alarm for some self-reflection?

"Have I become so 'for the church' that I am no longer 'for the Lord'?" is a valuable question to ask oneself at times. "Have I become so 'for the church' that I am no longer 'for the family'?" As we all know, kids develop a wart or two as they are growing up; the wedding day sheen on a spouse dulls. Slipping into more and more church activity to avoid the seamier side of family life can be a subconscious gesture complicating the need to face reality.

If the ABC's say that church has come to mean more to me than family, discernment is called for, preferably with a skilled person not tied to one's local church community. The counseling mode, often available to members of religious orders and to diocesan priests as a means for helping them understand more clearly the role of "for the church" in their lives, can be fruitful for lay ministers.

A valuable guide for discerning *for the church* can be found in the New Testament. In the earliest church, aspects relevant to contemporary ministry are: love, service, community, through the sharing of gifts and talents.

1. Love

"What I command is that you love one another." In John's gospel, Jesus speaks these words at the Last Supper. Loving one another seems to be the root from which all else will flourish in the church. In Acts, authored by Luke, we find that "the whole group of believers was united heart and soul; no one claimed for his own anything he had" (Acts 4:32). Loving one another is a fruit of the Spirit of God being in us and bringing us into community. In the First Letter to the Corinthians, Paul tells us that love surpasses even faith and hope. Love is also related to witness and evangelization, the intent of the verse "See how they love one another."

It sounds quite simple and quite beautiful. But is it? If the first requisite of being for the church is enabling the church to be a community, a community composed of persons who love one another, then the lay minister seems called to consider how his or her ministry contributes to a deepening of love within the whole. For example, a loving attitude toward the children in her care may be a more essential trait for a religious educator than concern about whether the children learn their lessons. On the other hand, the teacher who *does* love those in his or her care will, because of this love, provide setting, style, and subject matter through which the youngsters can learn.

Although enhancing love within the community is never the responsibility of any one person, it is still profitable for the lay minister to reflect for a while on: "In what ways has my minister been designed by my local parish to enhance love, and its fruit, community?"

2. Service

From the beginning to the end, from his healings to his washing of the feet at the Last Supper to his crucifixion, Jesus' ministry of serving others shines through. Consequently, in the early church, service was valued. To be *for the church* meant to be willing to serve the members of the church and the church as a whole community. Time and energy and organization were dedicated to that purpose, as we discover in the Acts of the Apostles and Paul's epistles.

In recent times, many lay people have welcomed the emergence of ministries in the church for the tangible service these provide. Ministry has enabled the expression of the powerful desires to serve often found in the hearts of the laity.

Serving one another in a local church, however, does not further community when those doing ministries form cliques or when factions emerge within a parish setting. No matter how hard lay ministers may work at accomplishing their tasks, they are not "for the church" in its service dimension if the call to love another is forgotten. Like the plague, the martyr syndrome is to be avoided, i.e., I should be loved because I-work-so-hard-for-the-church.

It may be helpful if those engaged in voluntary service remind professional staff, including clergy, that quantity of work and quality of service do not form a natural equation. We pity the unfortunate family with a mother who scrubs the knuckles off her hands getting the floor clean but who never has the time to listen to a child, or the energy to hug the child, because her heart is committed to clean floors rather than children. A church peopled with ministers who work so hard a smile is an effort instead of a spontaneous gesture of affection deserves the same pity for its lack of members truly willing to serve, to be for the church by building community.

Quantity versus quality is an issue for all the designated ministers in the community. For example, the home visitor who skips a visit here or there, or squeezes in a quick visit between shopping and a dentist appointment, yet who is insistent on keeping her roster of homes because she "doesn't want to hurt anyone's feelings," would be served by feedback from other lay ministers on the meaning of service.

3. Community

The third aspect of "for the church" reveals why love and service are necessary. In his First Epistle to the Corinthians, Paul envisions the community formed by the exercise of various gifts. The Spirit, according to Paul, "distributes different gifts to different people." In unison, the church can reflect the harmony that the body reveals when all of its diverse parts work together with no one part esteemed over another, and with all parts hurting when one part is injured. Each ministry is based on gift and no ministry is to be thought of as more necessary than another.

As mentioned before, being *for* can mean rallying to the defense *of.* Where love, service, and affirmation of gifts abound, rallying to the defense is invested *in the community as a whole* enabled by the Spirit and not in one or another person, group or faction within the community.

Whether we speak of the United Nations or of the family to which we belong, to encourage diversity means giving attention to the atmosphere in which the diversity is encouraged. Without love for one another, without the impulse to serve one another as well as the whole community, sharing gifts can flounder. Jealousies, resentments, and slanders easily creep into a group that values tasks and efficiency over community. Not necessarily motivated by malice, the seeds for disvaluation and subsequent dissension can be sown in subtle ways. Ministries enabled by the Spirit are called to *inter-relationship,* with each particular ministry working in a way that lends pleasure to the other ministries because *inter-relationship,* rather than individualism, is stressed within the community. Thus the usher who welcomes the people with a hospitality that is genuine helps their hearts become open to the word read by the lector and preached by the priest. The lector who reads with clarity and expression and feeling helps the people to hear the meaning and depth of the Lord speaking through the word, sowing seeds that the Lord will reap when the eucharistic minister offers the Communion bread or cup to the people. The inter-relationship of ministers engaging in love and service during the liturgy upbuilds the community which is offered to God for greater service beyond its sanctuary.

Community is directly related to spirituality. When community is non-existent, when factions reign and war with one another, personal prayer becomes privatized rather than poured out for the good of all. The affinity between spirituality and inter-relationship must be reinforced in an ongoing way.

The virtues of a parish that is a community alive with the fruits of the Holy Spirit—service and love—cannot be repressed. As the saying goes, "word gets around." And it gets around not by boasting but by the real-life stories of its vitality that people in this given local church tell to the friends, relatives, and strangers beyond its borders.

For Oneself Is Not Selfish

For oneself—that might sound like it belongs on the other side of the tracks when we speak of ministry because being for oneself is often equated with selfishness. But must "for oneself" always be a mischief-maker?

When we turn to Scripture for help, we find that disciples turned to Jesus with a plea, "Increase our faith." Having some humility about one's own strengths, including the strength of one's faith, is a healthy way of being "for oneself." No person in the church is an endless reservoir of faith and energy. The well runs dry at times; not to admit this is to believe in oneself as superhuman or, conversely, as so lacking in worth that only super-doing gives permission for one's existence.

Not to be "for oneself" in its healthiest form can be messianic, to be in the grip of a subconscious perception that says "I am the salvation of this community." To say "I've got to do it or it won't get done at all," or to claim "It's got to be done by me or it won't get done the right way," is what my mother always called trying to be "holier than the Pope."

"It won't wash," another favorite saying of my mother's, applies here. And being messianic won't wash because it isn't loving, and it isn't serving, and it isn't letting the gifts and talents of a community be shared by *many*.

In Luke's gospel we hear that "on their return the apostles gave him (Jesus) an account of all they had done. Then he took them with him and withdrew to a town called Bethsaida where they could be by themselves" (Lk 9:10–11). There Jesus tended to the crowds and in the late afternoon to his disciples.

In another passage, Jesus says to his disciples, "Come, rest a while."

"Come, rest a while" is his message to today's disciples as well.

Take the time to put your feet up, or to splash in puddles made by a spring rain, or to stretch out on the couch and listen to the birds or to a symphony on the stereo or to the sound of your own snoring—and to the voice of Jesus saying, "Come, rest a while—you deserve a time to be for yourself."

One can tend to tasks in a spirit of "dead on one's feet," but one cannot genuinely minister in that position. It's impossible to love, serve, and use one's gifts to the fullness of their promise with a fearful or angry or numb or cold or tired heart.

"Come, rest a while" is ultimately being, not only for oneself, but also for the church and for the Lord.

From Complements For

Ministry is not a self-appointed profession. Being for God, for the church, and for oneself needs to be complemented by a perception that one's ministry is *from God, from the church,* and *from oneself.*

In a time characterized by some as the "age of the laity" it is easy to overlook the fact that it is Jesus who calls and Jesus who sends. We minister, enabled by the Spirit, *from* his empowerment. Because of this, ministry is always a spiritual issue as well as a practical church and pastoral issue.

The *from* element of ministry is not meant to be intimidating. "Do not hide your light under a bushel," Jesus warns us. The laity need to be aware that the "who's who" concerning ministry in the gospel is not as clear as one might think. For example, there is confusion about the Twelve. Thaddeus is mentioned in Mark and Matthew but not in Luke or John. Luke has two Judases. John lists only eleven apostles, not citing Judas Iscariot. Peter, James, and John seemed to be particularly close to Jesus, being present at the transfiguration, the raising of Jarius' daughter, and Gethsemane.

According to the Jerome Biblical Commentary, we find the word apostle on Jesus' lips only once during the public ministry. And, in the early church, we find that apostle was a term of reference that went beyond the original Twelve. The following were also called apostles in the New Testament: James the "brother" of the Lord, Barnabas, Andronicus, and Junias whom some early church figures such as John Chyrsostom thought was a woman.

Jesus' sending out witnesses of his resurrection to preach the good news is the foundation of the apostolate (JBC 78:177).

But St. Paul, who was not at the resurrection, became an apostle. And it is through Paul's epistles that we discover the force of life found in being a missionary. Though Paul was not part of Jesus' original group, and may never have spoken with Jesus, he provides a significant model for ministry through the apostle-missionary channel.

Regarding ministry, Jesus was more generous of heart than his followers. John, in consternation, once said to him, "Master, we saw a man casting out devils in your name and because he is not with us, we tried to stop him." Jesus replied, "You must not stop him; anyone who is not against you is for you" (Lk 9:49–50).

Those are encouraging words for the lay minister whose ministry seems to bear fruit but who has misgivings about whether it is proper for the laity to be designated as ministers.

In Scripture, *discipleship is the fundamental relationship for ministry*. Therefore, in spite of the "who's who" confusions in Scripture about apostle, what ministry itself should mean is amply described by Jesus. The gospels, in fact, can be viewed as a school for ministry taught by Jesus. In passage after passage, events remembered by the earliest communities portray Jesus as instructing, challenging, encouraging, cajoling his followers.

In addition to the direct passages and references to ministry such as those found in chapter ten of Luke and Matthew, there are many other passages where we find Jesus giving instruction about faith, the bedrock for ministry and for the formation process for mission. We even see Jesus, like many teachers, at times experiencing "the last straw" because his disciples fail to learn the essence of what he has to teach. In Mark, chapter eight, for example, after the second miracle of the loaves, we sense Jesus' impatience with those who have answered his call.

Jesus and the disciples, by boat, go to another region. Jesus alone disembarks and is immediately confronted by Pharisees wanting a sign. Mark relates Jesus' discouragement explicitly: "And with a sign that came straight from the heart he said, "Why does this generation demand a sign? I tell you solemnly, no sign shall be given.'"

Back in the boat, Jesus warns his followers about the yeast of the Pharisees. Taking yeast in its literal sense, the disciples miss Jesus' meaning and remonstrate with one another about bread and the little provision to eat they have brought with them.

Jesus corrects them through a series of stinging questions directed at their lack of awareness in spite of what they have experienced in their own lives that very day:

> Why are you arguing? Do you not yet perceive or understand? Are your hearts hardened? Are your minds closed? Having eyes do you not see? Do you not remember? When I broke the five loaves among the five thousand, how many baskets full of scraps did you collect? When I broke the seven loaves for the four thousand, how many baskets full of scraps did you collect? Do you still not understand?

Jesus seems to be warning them not to become infected with arrogance as the Pharisees are. He is not angry about their lack of good will. But the task to which they are called demands more than good will; insights into the deeper meanings of what Jesus does and says are essential. Ministry is more profound than the evidence that meets the eye.

The passage ends abruptly with the last of Jesus' questions. The force of the interrogation makes any further explanation redundant. Reflection on one's lived experience, attention to Jesus' instruction, and fidelity to faith are essential for those who respond to the Lord's call. Some will witness without this; some will minister who are not as intimately a part of the community as the disciples; Jesus is as generous in ministry and witness as he is with loaves and fishes. Nonetheless, following means learning from Jesus; ministry means following in order to learn.

From the Church

Without Jesus, his example, his teaching, and his sending, there would be no rationale for ministry. Because of this, a perception that ministry is from the Lord should not be side-stepped in favor of a perception that one's ministry is "from the church." To cling to "from the Lord" and avoid "from the church" likewise distorts reality.

Ministry is an activity of the church and takes place, often, in the church—our common sense alone tells us that. What may be less clear is an understanding of how the call to ministry comes *from the church,* the institution as well as the local community.

Here in the United States light has been shed in recent years by the institutional church on the matter of lay ministry. In 1980, for the fifteenth anniversary of Vatican II's Decree on the Laity, the National Conference of Catholic Bishops provided a pastoral statement, *Called and Gifted: Catholic Laity 1980,* for reflection by other members of the church. *Called and Gifted* affirmed the emergence of the lay people into ministry:

> We acknowledge gratefully the continuing and increasing contributions of volunteers and part-time workers who serve on parish and diocesan councils, boards of education, and financial, liturgical and ecumenical committees, as well as those who exercise roles such as special minister of the eucharist, catechist and pastoral assistant. We are grateful, too, for the large numbers of lay people who have volunteered and are serving in the missions.[1]

The hierarchy, applauding the "solidarity between laity and clergy" which bears the fruit of "effective ministry and witness to the world," remind clergy and laity:

> Baptism and confirmation empower all believers to share in some form of ministry. Although the specific form of participation in ministry varies according to the gifts of the Holy Spirit, all who share in this work are united with one another.[2]

> We are convinced that the laity are making an indispensable contribution to the experience of the people of God and that the full import of their contribution is still in a beginning form in the post-Vatican II church.[3]

Passages from Vatican II documents are basic for perceiving lay ministry as emanating from the church in an organic way, for the church itself is a living organism, a pilgrim people of God. For example,

> As sharers in the role of Christ the priest, the prophet, and the king, the laity have an active part to play in the life and activity of the church. (AA 10)

> From the reception of these charisms of gifts, including those which are less dramatic, there arise for each believer the right and the duty to use them in the church and in the world for the good of humankind and for the upbuilding of the church. (AA 30)

The active role in the church that the laity are invited to engage in is not to be accomplished at the expense of their dignity as *lay* persons. That dignity, affirmed over and over in the Decree on the Laity, emerges from the very web of existence in which the lay life is rooted.

> But the laity, by their very vocation, seek the kingdom of God by engaging in temporal affairs and by ordering them according to the plan of God. They live in the world, that is, in each and in all of the secular professions and occupations. They live in the ordinary circumstances of family and social life, from which the very web of their existence is woven. (LG 4)

By becoming active within the church as lay persons, the laity bring the life of the secular world into the life of the church.

> Well-informed about the modern world, the lay person should be an active member of his own society and be adjusted to its culture. (AA 6)

> The laity should accustom themselves to working in the parish in close union with their priests, bringing to the church community their own and the world's problems as well as questions concerning human salvation, all of which should be examined and resolved by common deliberation. (AA 3)

As they become active in voluntary ministry within the church, some lay persons seem to "trade in" the secular world for the church world and let themselves become *churchified.* The fruit of this is often restlessness and unhappiness, for this kind of lay minister lives in limbo. On the one hand, he or she disdains or disowns the secular world (what has, in many ways, shaped the person's identity); on the other hand, the *totality* of church identity sought always eludes the person's grasp because in reality for the voluntary minister it does not exist.

From Oneself

The problem, and sometimes tragedy, of the full-time voluntary minister will not be overcome until lay men and women realize that "the laity consecrate the world itself to God."

What we are beginning to see is a pattern that warns against putting "all one's eggs in one basket." "From the Lord" and "from the community and institution of the church" form a *combination* that disallows foisting oneself as a voluntary minister onto the community and institution of the church. In a like way, ministry must not be foisted onto an individual lay person, though when I hear a late summer draft from the pulpit for religious education teachers, I have to remind myself that call, not coercion, is the intention of the church and the Lord. What this means is that the impulse for ministry must come also *from oneself.* In some cases, clergy and other professional staff persons may encourage and invite laity to volunteer their gifts in the service of ministry, but beyond invitation is the land where angels fear to tread. The "age of the laity" does not mean an age of dumping all the work in a parish onto the lap of the laity, using the word minister as a means for crossing off chores on a laundry list of "what this parish needs done in the next six months," decided by others than those who will do the work.

With Complements For and From

The last preposition in our formula is the most elusive. In various ways, aspects of "for" and "from" are rather explicitly spelled out in programs for lay ministries, in adult education, and in preaching. Concepts related to *with God, with the church,* and *with others* have received less adequate attention.

That God is with me when I minister is sometimes only faintly felt because of what some of us bring to ministry: an internal overemphasis of ministering *for* God. Too many of us still cling emotionally to a Jehovah concept of God as the One who demands obedience and who limits his action to judgment. From this, we fall into the mistaken view that ministry is something *we go away from God to accomplish for God.* Childishly, we believe that if we do it perfectly, God will be pleased and appeased. If we make mistakes, God will be disappointed and disapproving. Timidity may result.

"O ye of little faith," as Jesus once said when the boat was tipsy-turvy on the high seas. What we need in order to provide a rudder and anchor for our ministries is an increased faith that God is *with us as we minister.*

When a lay minister becomes conscious of the need *for* this companionship and alert to what Jesus teaches about it in the gospels, there is a greater probability that it will be experienced.

In the story of the disciples on the road to Emmaus in Luke's gospel (24:13–35), after Jesus vanishes from the sight of Cleopas and his friend Simon, the two men say to one another, "Did not our hearts burn within us as he talked to us on the road and explained the scriptures to us?" The stranger who accompanied them from Jerusalem to Emmaus, who asked them questions, who revealed a deeper understanding of God's word tied to the events of their own lives, who entered their lodging and shared their food was not recognized for who he was until he pronounced the blessing and broke the bread. Fortunately, when recognition did come, Cleopas and Simon acknowledged it, shared it with one another, and felt impelled to share it with the larger community.

This passage provides wonderful insights for lay ministers. It teaches us that sensing God's companionship can bring consolation where there is desolation. It helps us realize that God can be present where we perceive what is human, natural, and ordinary, i.e., those to whom we minister even though they be strangers and those with whom we walk the road of ministry. It helps us to appreciate inner responses, "our hearts burning within," and to notice these as indicators of where we sense the Holy. It nourishes our faith by pointing out that God's companionship is there whether we recognize it or not.

And it invites us to reflect on our ministerial encounters. So often we let the curtain for the final act fall as soon as a task is accomplished, as soon as we've spoken the last word of the first reading, or listened to the last insight from a child in religious education class, or ended our visit to the imprisoned or the infirm. The road to Emmaus encourages us to linger a while with the experience and discover where we have met the Lord on our particular road. It may aid us in understanding that when we go to church on Sunday, it's not our first encounter with God in a week; the Spirit has been with us as we minister to friends and family members of our parish, and the Spirit comes with us as we join others in worship.

There are several ways for us to become more aware that our ministry happens *with* the Spirit. *Scripture, prayer, and sharing together* can help us become alert to our companions in ministry. In the gospels we find Jesus pointing this out on a number of occasions. In Matthew's account of Jesus describing the mission of his disciples, we find not only an inventory of the work of disciples, but also indications of how God will be present in their ministry: "the Spirit of your Father will be speaking in you" when persecutions come (10:20); "you are worth more than hundreds of sparrows" so why be afraid? (10:31); "I will declare myself for you (disciples) in the presence of my Father in heaven" when you declare yourself for me (10:32); "anyone who welcomes you welcomes me; and those who welcome me welcome the one who sent me" (10:40).

It can be a consolation to those in voluntary ministry, who might be intimidated by others with more expertise, to hear Jesus say that God reveals himself to those disciples who minister: "I bless you, Father, Lord of heaven and of earth, for hiding these things from the learned and the clever and revealing them to mere children" (Mt 11:25–27).

The gospel is filled with surprises, but few perhaps are as sobering as chapter 25 in Matthew where we find Jesus saying that he will be in the stranger whom we welcome, the naked whom we clothe, the hungry whom we feed, the sick and the imprisoned whom we visit. Like Simon and Cleopas, we might not recognize Jesus in those we meet along the road unless we dwell for a while on that promise of presence Jesus has made to us. We can easily fall into self-absorption (worrying or glorifying about how unlike or like Jesus I am as a minister) and become blind to the *presence of Jesus* in those to whom we minister.

To live by the promise of Jesus means to live with a growing awareness of how intimately present the Spirit of God is within us in our lives and through our ministries. The people of God ministering in Jesus' name is a concept that became lost through the ages, replaced by laity as workers in the church; revived in our time in the many ministries exercised by the people, it reveals to us the condition church is called to be. In other words, the norm for church is a *people knowing the presence and work of God in their lives and bearing the fruit nurtured by this.*

Some lay ministers have found that they more fully realize the presence of God *as* they minister if they take the time to pray with God *before* they minister:

> Each week, before work in a soup kitchen sponsored by her parish, Elizabeth spends some time in silence and prayer, asking God to deepen her awareness of the promise to be in those whom she will serve.

Steve stumbled on this kind of prayer by accident.

> One Sunday, believing there would be a meeting before Mass, he arrived a half-hour before liturgy. The meeting had been postponed, so Steve sat in the sanctuary near the altar, meditating on the first reading, which he would soon proclaim to the community. That Sunday Steve noticed that he felt a greater sense of God's power in the word as he lectored and then listened to the gospel and the homily. After that, Steve made it a point to come to Mass early each week, whether or not he was the lector, in order to reflect on the word and God's presence in it.

Besides Scripture and prayer, sharing is a way to deepen one's sense of the presence of God as a companion, as one who walks beside and dwells within the one who ministers. By "going over" one's experience in ministry, in a comfortable fashion, with another person, the lay minister often finds beneath surface meanings a depth not noticed in the actual experience.

With the Church

Most lay ministers don't have to be told they are ministering *"with the church"*; the presence of other groups close by within the Church is a common experience and sometimes perceived as a mixed blessing.

Off-season, so to speak, we can step back and savor the quantity and quality of involvement in the parish, taking delight in knowing that one's ministry is accompanied by many ministries and that we have many colleagues in ministry.

Our reflection on *ministering with the Church* may include diocesan and universal church levels as well as the local level. As lay ministers we are part of a living organism whose gathered ministries provide witness and enable mission that thrusts forward a God-loved world.

As the renewal evoked by Vatican II bears fruit, visible and concrete bondings beyond the local church are emerging. For example, here in the Boston Archdiocese, at the vicariate or regional level, through the sponsorship of Bishop Daniel Hart, the CHRISM program encourages laity from the parishes in the Brockton region to come together. Effectively and sensitively guided by Sr. Florita Rodman, CHRISM enables quality adult education by combining into groups interested lay persons from a number of neighboring parishes.

The Buffalo, New York diocese provided for me an outstanding experience concerning ministering "with the church." After attending a religious education conference at Niagara Falls, my husband and I were invited to a banquet celebrating religious education teachers in the diocese. Sitting at a table with three couples from a local parish, we felt instantly welcomed and established easy rapport by sharing stories of family and experiences of ministry. At the end of the delicious meal, the master of ceremonies called forward from each table the lay man or woman who had been named religious educator of the year by a vote taken in the lay minister's parish. At the podium the award winner received a citation from the bishop. Uplifted by the enthusiasm around us, my husband and I cheered the recipient from our table as if we were lifelong members of his parish. The standing ovation given at the end of the ceremony for these faithful ministers of God was for me also a standing ovation for those who had originated and planned this yearly celebration for those engaged in the ministry of handing on the faith to the coming generation through religious education. Events such as the one in Niagara help the laity perceive that their shared ministry happens *with the church,* and that church means much more than what goes on here at Sacred Heart, or Holy Trinity, or St. Mary's.

With One Another

A different sense of "with" regarding ministry, one that operates on a more personal level, is evoked when persons with similar interests gather regularly to share and pray with one another. Sometimes this can be effectively accomplished across parish borders as well as within them. My favorite instance of this involves three women who originally met four years ago when each participated in a year-long program of preparation for the voluntary ministry of spiritual direction. After the program ended, Sue, Nancy, and Gerry responded to a mutual desire to gather monthly to reflect on spirituality and spiritual dynamics of ministry. Each was from a different setting—one from an urban parish, one from a suburban parish, and one from a United Church of Christ parish. As time passed, they found a freedom in sharing emerging in their group as an irreplaceable support because the parishioners and colleagues in ministry, in each particular locale, were not known to the two other members of the group.

"We can really let our hair down and be amazingly honest with one another in our feedback," Nancy explained. "This helps us be more open with God when we pray together. Being with Sue and Gerry, and knowing I can rely on them, is a breath of fresh air for me and my ministry."

This chapter has been an attempt to clarify basic elements of ministry in order to provide a theological foundation for understanding the dimensions of spirituality significant to ministry. The for–from–with device was used to reveal the connections and inter-relationships between ministry and God, the church and oneself.

If, in order to review the elements, we turn the prism, the shift we create may help us align the insights in a different sequence: looking at the lay minister for, from, and with God, looking at the lay minister for, from, and with the church, looking at lay ministry as for and from oneself and with others who also minister.

Reflecting on the lay minister's relationship with God, we discovered that being for God, by following Jesus, is primary to ministry. We learned that ministry that unfolds from this knowing and following can be fruitfully lived out in the web where we have woven our lives. Without the gospel and Jesus, ministry as we have come to know it would not have emerged as constitutive to the church. On the other hand, ministry is not an activity we can take for granted because we claim to follow Jesus and be for him; Jesus is the initiator. The call to ministry and the empowerment for ministry come from him through the Spirit to us. *Ministry is for and from God* through the One whom we call Lord, the One who said: "I will not leave you orphans." "I am with you always." "The Spirit will speak in you." "The Advocate, the Holy Spirit, will teach you."

In addition, *ministry happens with God.* We may minister to many different kinds of people, we may have a variety of colleagues (priests, brothers, sisters, and laity) who join us in ministry, but we also have as companion the One who is same and steadfast regardless of where we minister and to whom we minister.

Clarity concerning basic theological elements related to church was also an aim of this chapter. Within our culture there are a variety of ways to exercise charity—philanthropic organizations for example. These are significant to mission but are not usually identified as ministry. Ministry is a church-related activity. Because of this, the dynamics between the lay minister and the church deserve attention. In reflecting on these dynamics, I suggested that the fruits of a ministry that is *for the church* are love, service, and the sharing of gifts, all activated by the Holy Spirit in a way that enhances community.

Ministry is also *from the church.* To be for the church is to be for the community the church is called to be. But the institution, as well as the community, calls forth ministry. In our time and in our culture, Vatican II and the church leadership in the United States have reminded the laity that, through baptism and confirmation, they are empowered to minister. The bishops of the United States have affirmed laity who live out that empowerment.

The hope of many is that where we today see institution, we eventually will also see community. For example, Bishop Neves of the Pontifical Council of the Laity in the Vatican has suggested that the church can live fully and be a perfect sign among peoples, only when the hierarchy and the laity are working in mutuality, and the hierarchy incorporates laity working with them. Bishop Neves' conviction is that the church is incomplete without the presence, ministry, and efforts of the laity.

If church is both community and institution, and if our ministry in the church is called to enhance a sense of community through love and service, then a consciousness of ministering *with the church,* companioned by colleagues who also minister, nurtures the desire that one's ministry be a reconciling donation to the upbuilding of this community.

Does a church that is not a respecter of the personhood of its members deserve the name community? Schedules, no matter how slavishly served, don't minister; persons do. With this in mind, we come to look at ourselves as ministers and to consider *respect for one's own needs* for nourishment of mind, heart, spirit, and body. In the long run this kind of respect contributes to the way one ministers and goes about building community. Seeing oneself, occasionally, as seated by the well, saying "I am parched" as Jesus did, helps one realize that ministry and humanness are friends, not enemies.

Self-respect means that one will appreciate choice and will resist trendiness and coercion into particular ministries by reflecting on what gifts the Spirit has bestowed that could be given in response to a call, affirmed by the church, but originating in the Lord.

The kind of self-respect that characterizes mature adulthood does not flourish without a valuation placed on horizontal elements suggested by community and gifts. The choices lay persons make about church are choices about isolation or community. Two friends, John and Primm ffrench, could easily have opted for isolation. Both are artists who could have made and sold batik vestment and silk-screened banners. Instead, they threw their lot in with the Vineyard and encouraged the community to express its faith through the arts. Evoking communal creativity is an arduous task; it has meant that John and Primm take time during each liturgical season to enable the members of the community to create a fitting symbolic expression of the season such as a twelve foot paper mosaic angel for Christmas, an evolving icon of the earth for Advent, and an appliquéd altar cloth and wall hanging for Easter. One season, guided by John and Primm, individuals and families created twenty-five wall hangings which were later shared with neighboring parishes. Outreach beyond their local community to the broader church was also accomplished through the presentation of workshops on the creative arts and faith and through exhibits displaying the creativity of the community.

In this example, we see a range of specific behaviors evoked by "being for" referred to in this chapter. I suggest this range of specific behaviors as a necessary antidote to the passive and vague pleasantness that can sometimes substitute for relationship with God and for community in the church.

Triological fits the dynamic described in these chapters. One of the clearest examples of the triological versus the dialogical is the infant playing with a rattle. If another person is part of the process, the baby responds to the gestures and voices of this person who, in turn, responds to the infant's gurgles and discoveries made while exploring the rattle. Alone with the rattle, the baby quickly becomes bored. The texture of the experience is enriched and animated when the communication is three-way.

In the gospel, we also see a triological dynamic—with the disciples, Jesus points to mission; with the crowds, Jesus points to the kingdom; with the Father, Jesus points to the people and the events at hand.

The triological is at the foundation of our belief system, for Catholics believe in a three-personed God who is one in unity and nature.

As we respond to the call for unity with God, unity with the church, and unity within oneself in its psychological and spiritual sense, what maturity of faith means comes to light. Unity with God that lacks the inclusion of others becomes arid, unity with the church without a sense of mission to the world become stultifying, unity within oneself that does not evoke love and service poured out for others is not lasting.

"Come and see," invites Jesus. No matter which way we look at Jesus, what we see is love as the fruit of mutuality *with* faith *for* the sake of a loved world, community *with* disciples, and a sending *from* that community *for* the sake of that loved world.

PART TWO

8

READYING THE SOIL FOR MINISTRY

A friend of mine recently made a week-long retreat in part to discern whether to let go of leadership within the ministry of music in her parish to accept an invitation to serve on the diocesan liturgical and prayer commission. It was her first retreat since adolesence.

Her prayer times on the retreat were ups and downs, struggle and fears tinged at times with hope. Her eyes brightened, however, as she told me about a night toward the end of the retreat:

> I woke up one night about midnight. I forgot I wasn't at home and the pitch darkness of the room terrified me. I felt that I had fallen into a great abyss. After putting on the light and my robe, I left the room for a bit and walked up and down the corridor. When I returned, as I opened the door, I felt within myself this fullness, as if the emptiness inside me was being filled to overflowing. Suddenly I sensed a great peace within and all around me.

To my friend, this was the most powerful experience of her retreat. "What struck me," she said, "was that it didn't happen while I was praying. The best spiritual experience of the retreat happened when I wasn't praying!" The fact that God was available and present even when she wasn't praying surprised and delighted her. And it taught her that God's availability and presence do not depend on us!

"The new way God came to me on retreat helped me to decide in favor of the new venture on the liturgical and prayer commission. It was like God was inviting me to grow, to accept a new challenge. But I'd like to understand what happened. Can you help me with that?"

"Well, we can look at it one of two ways," I replied. "We can see it as Abbot André Louf does and say that for a believer the heart is already in a state of prayer but one's consciousness may lack awareness of this. Or we can begin to perceive spirituality as something that is not limited to times of prayer. We can call what happened to you a religious experience. When we do that, then we may begin to look at other life experience besides prayer as a place where God may reveal something significant to us."

"But that's what happens to me over and over with music! Now I see how much I needed that experience on the retreat in order to serve on the liturgical and prayer commission. Until then I didn't even recognize all the times music had led me into spiritual experience. Understanding that will be crucial to developing new ways music can be used to encourage spirituality in the diocese."

To perceive that prayer is the only religious experience available to us contradicts both the Old and New Testaments. Paul on the road to Damascus, the woman filling her water jar at the well, Mary Magdalene at the tomb, the disciples on the road to Emmaus, Jacob after passing over the ford of Jaboc, Moses tending the flock on Mount Horeb, Mary consoled by her cousin and friend Elizabeth—each had a powerful religious experience.

That "on the road" may be the place to look for God is an insight spoken of earlier in this book. Put another way, developing a contemplative attitude, recognizing moments, in Rudolf Otto's words, when we encounter the "mysterious tremendum" and the "mysterious fascinans," protects our spirituality from becoming repetitive and shallow, something to be slighted or an insincere "saying the lines."

Reflecting quietly on some of our ordinary experiences, some that may emerge from our ministries, for example, but particularly those experiences that "stay with us" during a week or month, can help us become aware of how we actually *do* exercise our spiritual dimension and how sometimes we pray without realizing we are in prayer. One lay minister who learned to do this now calls spirituality "a great adventure."

In many ways, this book is about making distinctions, not for the sake of rigidity but for the sake of clarity and understanding about spirituality and ministry. The most common trouble many spiritual directors encounter in trying to help believers is the conviction within the believer that spirituality and prayer are synonomous.

Patterns of Spiritual Behavior

Let's take a look at a very ordinary experience—that of contemplating a newborn baby. While we do this we can consider the three reactions of three parishioners who are helping Jerry and Maria prepare for baby Jill's baptism. The incident takes place the first time that Ed, Anne, and Lillian, ministers within the baptism program, see Jill.

Ed, on seeing the baby, whoops, "Hey, Jerry, she's going to be a redhead, just like you!"

When the blanket is removed and Jill begins to kick her tiny legs, Anne exclaims, "She is soooo beautiful! God bless her!"

Lillian, standing between Ed and Anne, sighs, "Ohhhhhh." Later that evening, while clearing dishes from the table at home, Lillian remembers the baby, savors her and wishes she had held her in her arms. She senses the fragility of infancy and the honor it is to be a minister of baptism. Then Lillian refers the baby to God, asking God to watch over Jill with heartfelt care.

What is happening to Ed, Anne, and Lillian? Ed's pattern is one of *noticing* rather than absorption. He became aware of one fact about the baby in the immediate moment of seeing her, and he related it to Jerry without any reference to God. Most of us frequently function this way, a way that is a natural attribute of being human, of exercising a spiritual zest for life.

Anne became *absorbed* in the baby and *spontaneously articulated* this to God. If you ask Anne tomorrow what she said when she saw Jill, she might not be able to tell you because at the moment of seeing the baby her awareness of herself was not apparent. Here we have one of those blessed times when we are startled into a sudden linking of God with a life event. It's easy to belittle our "God bless" moments but it's folly to overlook them, as they are part and parcel of how we function as spiritual persons.

Totally absorbed, Lillian was *caught up in* the *awe* of the moment. After a delay, *awareness* came, accompanied by desire and *articulation* about the infant to God. This is a common pattern we exercise in regard to prayer. We become caught up in savoring an experience. Later we remember it, reflect on it, and refer it to God. If we keep in mind that both instances are religious experiences, we enrich our understanding of spirituality. Lillian had a religious experience when she first saw Jill. Lillian had a religious experience later in the evening when she explicitly referred this experience to God.

Most believers realize that a relationship with God calls for a foundation more solid than prayer evoked only by an event in life drawing us into prayer. On the other hand, reflecting on those encounters that "stay with us" and encouraging prayer to unfold from the memories brings a vibrancy into prayer. Setting aside time for this kind of reflection and prayer may be difficult, but people who manage to do this notice its fruits in everyday life. This evidence encourages them to set aside contemplative times at least once or twice a week.

A Primer on Prayer

Just as preparing for ministry usually involves aspects of education, understanding the basic elements of prayer can be reinforced by reviewing a brief primer on prayer. One afternoon Sheila, a lay minister friend, and I put our heads together about such a primer for those in ministry. Sheila suggested the following ABC's to initiate the project:

A. Prayer is not a substitute for ministry.
B. Ministry is not a substitute for prayer.
C. Prayer and ministry go hand in hand.

My response was that her ABC's were a bit obvious. She then teased me about mutual friends who had yet to *learn* these ABC's. While we were engaged in "back to basics," I reminded her that (a) thinking about God is not prayer, (b) thinking about prayer is not prayer, and (c) thinking about ministry is not prayer.

"In other words, a rose is a rose is a rose," Sheila replied with a chuckle. "If prayer is prayer is prayer, what *are* the ABC's of *basic* prayer?"

"I'll take on your challenge! Prayer is always relational. Prayer is addressed to or is directed toward Another. Prayer is always affective."

"By affective, you mean that prayer engages our feelings?" Sheila went on answering her own question. "In other words, prayer is an activity of the heart directed outward to One who is loved."

"Most of the time loved." I added this in an effort to be accurate. "Prayer *isn't* if it isn't honest."

"In a nutshell—prayer is the *real* God and the *real* person having an encounter aligned with reality."

"Making prayer a religious experience." We pondered how we had backed into this insight and why we both felt these basic things had to be said, agreeing that the impulse came from knowing instances from our own lives when our activity was often:

to sit and reflect without directing the reflection toward God;

to let the affective dimension emerge but not express the affect to God;

to let the affective dimension emerge, e.g., sadness, compassion, anger, but to grow introspective or analytical or repressive rather than relational;

to address God but to suppress the feeling level while doing that.

When I suggested to my cohort that she could write this primer better than I could, she gracefully urged that we collaborate on discerning why men and women who participate in ministry need to pray. Together we came across six reasons:

1. The Need to Know One's Connections

Both Sheila and I had had the experience of buying Christmas presents in July, hiding them in the closet till the holiday, then, in December, discovering that we had forgotten for whom we had purchased the gifts. The analogy to ministry is that without an ongoing and active spirituality, the focus of the minister may fall on immediate functions or on the everyday activity of the parish or school. The One who is the source and meaning of the ministry as well as the value of the community can seem as distant as July from December.

The "church-connection" before long overwhelms the "God-connection."

Ministry is God-connected. If ministry remains prayer-connected, there's more than an even chance that an awareness of this primary connection will stay intact. Without the prayer connection, the minister may have less spiritual vitality than the people for whom the ministry is intended.

2. The Need To Dialogue with One's Companion

Prayer enables a sense of solidarity with Jesus and/or the Spirit as the lay person ministers. Dialogue with this Companion assists in preventing a sense of failure and isolation when one is discouraged and a sense of conceit when one finds one's ministry enabling others. The mutuality that sharing with God in prayer evokes deepens the minister's awareness that God is at work, accompanying the minister and laboring through his or her efforts.

3. The Need for Nourishment Along the Way

> He said to me, "You are my servant
> in whom I shall be glorified";
> while I was thinking, "I have toiled in vain,
> I have exhausted myself for nothing" (Is 49:3-4).

Affirmation nourishes. When affirmation similar to that expressed by the prophet Isaiah is sensed in prayer, the heart is energized forward even when fatigue seems to overwhelm the one who ministers. Without spiritual nourishment along the way, thirst and hunger weaken the minister and enervate the ministry.

4. The Need for Guidance

Few would claim that education for ministry is completed in the preparatory period. As ministry moves along, questions arise, new situations pose the need for direction. Brought to prayer, the questions and new situations may be guided by insights that emerge in prayer. These insights will need consultation and testing, but letting God tutor while on the road of ministry is far better than "going it alone," for the one engaged in ministry and for the Church community.

5. The Need To Celebrate

When children respond enthusiastically to the lesson presented by a religious educator, when a grieving widower sobs openly and freely with a minister of the bereaved, when an inner healing is perceived by a hospital visitor, relief or gladness of heart is spontaneous and often accompanied by the urge to share. Respect for confidentiality rightfully inhibits naming names and sharing the event even with family, close friends, and clergy. The right move is the move into prayer and celebration with God.

6. The Need To Share Sorrow

When prayer and ministry are in tandem, turning to God becomes as natural as talking to a dear friend. In one's ministerial encounters, if the heart becomes laden with sorrow, the consolation that only God can give will readily be sought in prayer, reviving hope and faith within the minister.

Co-Workers of God

In Corinth, in the early Christian community there, quarrels erupted, factions emerged. To quell the trouble, the apostle

Paul, in an epistle, interprets the trouble as rivalry based on a perception of belonging to particular ministers rather than to the community and Christ:

> This is what I mean: One of you will say, "I belong to Paul," another "I belong to Apollos," still another "Cephas has my allegiance," and a fourth, "I belong to Christ." Has Christ then been divided into parts? (1 Cor 1:12–13).

Later in this letter to the Corinthians, Paul invites his hearers to look at the identity of the favored ministers:

> After all, who is Apollos? And who is Paul? Simply ministers through whom you became believers, each of them doing only what the Lord assigned. I planted the seed and Apollos watered it, but God made it grow. This means that neither he who plants nor he who waters is of any special account, only God who gives the growth. He who plants and he who waters work to the same end. . . . We are God's co-workers, while you are his cultivation, his building (1 Cor 3:5–9).

Being co-workers of God is perhaps the most essential reason for persons engaged in ministry to pray. An awareness of God, as we plant and as we water, gives assurance that it *is* God who gives the growth, diluting within us any messianic tendencies that inhabit the heart.

Paul asks the members of the Corinthian community and its ministers to reflect on what we call identity. Reflection of this order is the plow, in a sense, that readies the soil for the planting, the watering, the harvesting. In an earlier chapter, I invited the readers to look at the attitudes one brings to prayer—Who is God in prayer for me? Who am I in prayer? What do I bring to prayer?—attitudes that shape *spiritual identity.*

Plowing the Other Field

Plowing the soil also means reflecting on one's own *ministerial identity,* including attitudes about myself that I bring to ministry. Such reflection can unfold into the prayer characterized earlier as direct and heartfelt address to God.

The following inventory is *one* example of the kinds of reflective questions that a minister, setting aside some time for quiet solitude, can beneficially ask after requesting God to shed light on the answering process. A deepened sense of self goes hand in hand with prayer and with ministerial activity. The questions in the text are offered to stimulate other questions related to one's own particular ministry. Pondering *those* questions (your own questions), not in an analytical way, but in an open way that encourages the response to emerge from the heart and spirit, from feelings and insight, may deepen your awareness of yourself and your ministry and community.

We are called to love God with our whole mind, heart, and spirit, and to love neighbor as oneself. As this is the alpha and omega of faith, consideration of mind, heart, and spirit are the focus of the questions.

Mind

How am I taking responsibility for deepening my understanding of my particular ministry? For example, if I am a lector, am I taking the time to discover, through reading or courses, more about Scripture as God's word?

How am I taking responsibility for carrying out my particular ministry? For example, if I am preparing for the exercise of the ministry of lector, do I practice aloud before reading to the congregation? Do I take the time to check on pronunciation and to read exegesis of the passages? Am I open to feedback that critiques my performance?

Heart

What sensitivities do I feel toward those to whom I minister? If I am a lector, do I feel an urgency about the power of the word in people's lives? If I am a hospital visitor, how do I feel about the elderly and the ill? If I am a parish council member, do I feel a need to know the feelings and views of the parishioners?

What feelings do I bring to the *tasks* of my ministry? Do I begrudge the time? Do I wish for an expansion or a diminishment of my role?

What emotions do my colleagues in ministry awaken in me? Do I hanker for change or for "the way things used to be"?

How do I feel about God as I initiate my ministry, or now that I am engaged in ministry? Has ministry changed my perception of God? My feelings about God? My sense of God's proximity?

Am I becoming more aware of the feelings Jesus experienced in his ministry—his pity for the widow of Naim, his joy for the ministry of the seventy-two disciples, his sorrow over Jerusalem, his eagerness of heart in responding to the leper?

Is my heart sincere? Jesus was adamant against hypocrisy, against playing a role with a pretend heart. The challenge of this for church community and for the minister is not having as one's goal *trying* to care, but having a heart, enabled through prayer by the Spirit, that truly *does* care or has the courage and honesty to admit it doesn't care—at least to self and God. Reflecting with God on your sincerity, and sincerity within your church community, can be accomplished within the context of Scripture. For example, in Mark 7:7 we hear Jesus quote Isaiah:

> This people honors me only with lip-service,
> while their hearts are far from me.
> The worship they offer me is worthless,
> the doctrines they teach only human regulations.

In Matthew's account, Jesus, addressing the people and his disciples, castigates the scribes and the Pharisees for their "hypocrisy and vanity." Among the charges he levels are injunctions regarding sincerity:

> You, however, must not allow yourselves to be called Rabbi, since you have only one Master, and you are all brothers. You must call no one on earth your father, since you have only one Father, and he is in heaven. Nor must you allow yourselves to be called teachers, for you have only one Teacher, Christ. The greatest among you must be your servant. Anyone who exalts himself will be humbled, and anyone who humbles himself will be exalted (Mt 23:1–12).

Jesus realized how the combination of pride and power could cripple the heart. That may be why he not only refuted but also refused all temptations and opportunities to exercise pride and power. Within his own disciples and within his ministers today, he expects the same sincerity of heart.

Spirit

How does God minister to me? This is an essential question related to the spirituality of the lay minister for several reasons. If I, as a lay minister, claim to minister to others, then it is arrogance to make that claim unless I acknowledge that the Spirit ministers to me. Secondly, if our minds and hearts are engaged in ministry, so too is our spirit, a spirit that develops vibrancy for ministry through the attentive care given to us by the Spirit.

Some people resist the idea that God ministers to them; some resist naming the need to be ministered to.

A story may clarify these points better than analysis.

A priest once made a directed retreat. The director suggested that he pray with the story of the good Samaritan, imagining himself in the scene. The following day, he returned to the director and said he had been the good Samaritan in praying the passage.

The director then suggested that, for the following day, he pray the parable with himself as the peson in the ditch rescued by the good Samaritan. The retreatant looked puzzled but said he would give it a try.

This time when the priest returned, he looked glum. "Every time I hear this story I *always* picture myself as the good Samaritan. I can't be the man in the ditch. I'm neither needy nor wounded."

"Give it another try," urged the director.

Returning again, the retreatant looked even more glum. "It won't work. I *have* to be the good Samaritan!"

"All the time?" asked the director before she suggested that he give it one more try.

When he returned the following day, the priest sat down and sighed. "It worked," he said, sighing again. "Not when I was at prayer. Later in the evening. I was sitting staring at the blaze in the fireplace when all of a sudden between myself and the fireplace, I saw a ditch with me in it, crying out to God. I moved then into the chapel, and all my neediness,

buried deep inside for the past few years when I had to be
who I *said* I'd be instead of who I am, came surging up along
with a few tears."
That night, for the first time in his life, the priest let the Spirit
minister to him.

Those of us—priests, sisters, brothers, lay ministers—who
are less resistant welcome the ministrations of the Spirit. We
know our own private moments when God, through the Spirit,
has consoled, comforted, healed, and encouraged us to go on
with the journey. Contemplating these times is a step in readying
the soil for ministry, especially when the reflection unfolds into
gratitude expressed to God directly.

Of like benefit is contemplating self as part of the people of
the Church and asking, "As a member of the body of Christ, how
have I been open to the ministrations of God experienced in
Church community?"

Hearers of the Word

The people, including the lay ministers, are nourished by
the word; therefore, contemplating yourself as a hearer of that
word can be valuable. In the Old Testament stories, from the
invitation of the Beloved in the Song of Songs:

Come then, my love,
my lovely one, come.
For see, winter is past,
the rains are over and gone.
The flowers appear on the earth,
the season of glad songs has come ... (Sg 2:10–13)

to the invitation of Isaiah:

Come to the water,
all you who are thirsty (Is 55:1–3)

we are urged into relationship with God.

"Listen, anyone who has ears to hear," is the open invitation of Jesus in the New Testament. "Come, follow me." We

hear this call again and again if we have ears to hear. Responding as disciples, we realize that Jesus, through this invitation, is ministering, not mandating, when we hear, in John's gospel, Jesus calling those who have faithfully followed, "Friends, not servants"—friends of such intimacy that the image of branch and vine is used to describe the friendship.

In the Psalms we are reminded of how God ministers to us in this intimate relationship:

Your rod and your staff comfort me (Ps 23).
You shield me with your hand (Ps 139).

When we heed that invitation to relationship, experiencing, as answer to our response, God's saving love, we begin to move from looking at the word, to listening to the word, to loving the word, to living the word.

As part of the people of the Church, where am I on that continuum? Readying the soil means pondering that question.

All lay ministers, as mentioned earlier, are part of the people of the Church, the ecclesia, the body of Christ. *Within* the people, not isolated and apart from them, each of us is called to be a hearer of the word that revives and strengthens our spirit.

Nourished by Sacrament

In a like manner, as part of the people we are invited to be nourished by the sacraments. With the new flourishing of lay ministries, it is the misfortune of some to focus so on the role of minister and its activities that the sacramental life slips to second or third place along with the perception of any need for the nourishment of the Spirit.

By looking at the Church as revealer and nourisher of faith, we can begin to perceive that all ministries contribute to that revealing and nourishing as well as to healing, teaching, worshiping, evangelizing, governance, prophecy, and hospitality.

Although the sacraments, a sign of the unbounded generosity of God in our time, are in many ways not dependent on one's "situation" (economic, cognitive, or emotional), during special times of unique events and transitions—confirmation, marriage, holy orders—and during ordinary times of "human condition" events—penance, the sacrament of the sick—and as God's response to the changes and needs evoked by everyday life—the Eucharist—sacraments nourish us as mentioned earlier in the book. In order to nourish the spirits of the people, these sacraments need the context provided by all the ministries within the church community (teaching, healing, proclaiming, evangelizing, social outreach, etc.). In other words, all the lay ministers within the local community participate in the giving as well as the receiving.

Lay ministers involved in liturgical planning and eucharistic ministry may easily move into this kind of reflection. To appreciate, however, the interdependence of all persons and ministries within the body of Christ, others of us may need to reflect on Paul's First Letter to the Corinthians (12:12–14, 18–26), Paul's reflection on the body of Christ where he confirms that, though of many parts, we have the unity of one body in which all are needed and all are of equal concern. Other passages in Scripture can likewise help us deepen our sense of the nourishing quality of ministry and of the constancy of the Spirit as the One who responds to the need within the minister's spirit.

In preparing the spirit for ministry, each of us is invited to reflect on God ministering in a way similar to one's own ministry:

the minister of the sick or the bereaved—healing

the religious educator—teaching

the usher/greeter—inviting, welcoming

the parish council representative—leading, governing

the Christian service minister—serving

the social activist—prophesying

the lector—revealing

the eucharistic minister—nourishing

In addition, all ministers can find it fruitful to the spirit to reflect on any of the scriptural sources related to other ministries, for all ministries are interdependent. In particular, whatever one's ministry, contemplating the word and the sacraments vivifies the spirit, enabling one to move from listening to the word to loving the word to living the word.

Motivation

Why am I engaged in ministry?

Motivation for one's participation in ministry calls for reflection in much the same way as contemplating one's mind, heart, and spirit. If we perceive reflection as the plough preparing the soil, the stones and clumps of weeds that could mar our motives will be unearthed, examined, and eliminated, enabling the mind, heart, and spirit to respond with freedom to God's call and challenge and sustaining love.

One counter-stance that can infect motivaton is letting ministry become self-serving, using it to enhance one's own image in the community. I call that *the utilitarian stance.* In contrast is the *mature spiritual stance,* a dynamic in which one's reference point is beyond self, in which one's motif is service.

The utilitarian stance seeks status, signals superiority, and parades piety. Honest answers to the following questions can help one discern if one is using ministry to add a touch of glory to oneself.

Through my ministry, do I send mixed messages—e.g., hospitality on the one hand, elitism on the other? Am I concerned about my ministry improving my self-image?—about the empowerment over others ministry confers?—about wanting others to appreciate the fullness of my faith? Do I believe that if I serve the church, I will earn more love from the Lord?

If my motive is spiritually mature, affirmative answers will emerge as response to the following questions: Am I engaged in ministry because I love God and God's people? Am I developing greater sensitivity to the people instead of getting caught up in the details of my ministry? Do I love the people I serve more than I love my image of myself as a minister? Is my ministry helping me become more aware of the signs of the times beyond my local community instead of trapping me within the confines of the local community? Do I find desire growing within me to be part of a lay mission to the world?

If I share honestly with the Lord these reflections on mind, heart, spirit, and motive—if I listen to the Lord's response and let myself be converted to it—then I have readied the soil, and I am eager now to move into planting, watering, weeding, and watching the growth God enables.

Having suggested the value of contemplating oneself, I will now reflect on contemplation as an approach to life, ministry, and prayer.

9

PLANTING THE SEED—
CONTEMPLATIVE AWARENESS AND PRAYER

Getting perspective is something we all do. "Stand at the other end of the room so I can see if it really fits" is what I sometimes say to a daughter who has purchased a new dress or adjusted the hem on an old skirt. I need to get a perspective denied when she and I stand face to face. Going outside and standing in the street tells us whether the Christmas lights can be seen by people passing by. We can't determine that by standing next to the Christmas tree even if we stood there till Valentine's Day. In museums we back away from paintings in order to "really" see them. Front row seats in the theater aren't always the best seats in the house.

What I'm talking about, of course, is the "seeing the woods from the trees" phenomenon.

An inability to see the woods from the trees is why some people still pray in childish, unsatisfactory ways or develop problems in prayer, or pray with less depth than they desire. In this book we are "standing back" from the experience of our prayer and our ministry to get a better perspective on them. In this chapter on planting the seeds for our spiritual life as lay ministers of the Lord, we will set our sights on the contemplative approach to life, ministry and prayer and begin by reflecting for a moment on the word *approach.*

"When the boat approached the harbor, it began to sink." In this sentence *approach* means to draw near to something.

"The conductor took a modern approach to the symphony." *Approach* here refers to the means by which the conductor interpreted the symphony. Approach was not something that ended when the conductor reached the podium and lifted his baton. The way or style used throughout the symphony is the sense of the word *approach.*

Both meanings of approach are significant to a discussion of what is called the *contemplative approach.* Contemplative can refer to the disposition in which we enter prayer. It can also refer to the means (the how) utilized during the experience of prayer.

Other approaches or methods of prayer may be more familiar than contemplation. And it might be wise to look at what is more familiar to learn, by contrast, what may be less familiar.

Aretha Franklin's song, "Say a Little Prayer for You," became popular, perhaps, because it speaks about the most common form of prayer: petition. What day goes by when most of us don't ask God to do us a favor? Rushing to catch the bus I mumble, "Let me be on time, Lord." Knowing that lost hours not spent on homework may tell the tale, a student nonetheless whispers, "Please help me pass this exam, Jesus."

Even if we haven't heard the song "Say a Little Prayer for You," most of us have heard another person urge us to "say a little prayer for me." And often we take that *intention* to prayer, responding to the request by making a request of God.

Rote is another method of prayer used frequently. Whether it is the Jesus prayer, the Hail Mary, or the Our Father, *repetition* is often considered the value of rote prayers. Sometimes we use this approach as an aid to establishing a routine; other times we use this approach because we are desperate and cannot pray spontaneously because a situation has momentarily overwhelmed us. Rote prayer here is the life boat we use so we won't go down in that boat that's approaching the harbor.

Rote and petitionary prayer are valuable approaches to the Lord. Hardly a week goes by that I don't rely on one *and* the other. The contemplative approach is one more way to increase one's faith through prayer.

For a moment contrast the styles of rote and petition with what is going on in the following story:

> Around noon, before going down to fix some lunch at Weston, I put away my work, closed my eyes, and rested my head on the back of the chair. For two or three minutes, thoughts about possibilities for lunch and plans for the afternoon

danced together in my mind. Then I pushed them aside to listen to the quiet. It seemed as if total silence reigned over the world until an airplane flying overhead drew my attention. The sound of a splash made by a car hitting a puddle of melted snow blended with the whirr overhead. Then I heard the bang, bang, bang of a hammer alternating with the jagged, harsh sounds of a jackhammer. A voice called out a greeting to someone passing by. The sounds, though distinct, blended into melody that sang of life. A feeling of delight surged within. "How precious is your world, God!" I felt my own heart making sound in unison with the sounds in God's creation.

Contemplation engages the heart. In this instance, my heart became absorbed by the sounds of life outside my window, by the present moment of life I was experiencing. Past and future faded away. The pattern of the experience looked like this:

1. Closed my eyes.
2. Thought about lunch and afternoon. (Head went on working.)
3. Pushed the thoughts aside. (Exercised will against mind.)
4. Sensed the silence and listened to it.
5. Heard the plane, the splash, the hammer, the jackhammer, the voice. (With my eyes closed, my hearing became alert and made distinctions.)
6. I sensed a melody in the combined sounds. (My heart awakened. I felt delight.)
7. "How precious is your world, God." (My heart shared its feeling with God.)

At the end of these brief contemplative moments with the sounds outside my window, I left my office and went down the stairs anticipating lunch, feeling rested and restored. In a similar way, when I pray contemplatively about my ministry, often the prayer enables me to go forward with the ministry refreshed and renewed. I then anticipate its challenges and joys.

It might be helpful to linger a little longer with the experience just described in order to see how it differs from petitionary prayer. "Say a little prayer for me." "Let me be on time, Lord."

"Help me pass this test." In these instances the person approaches God with an *intention*. In my contemplative noon-time experience, there was no particular intention at work when I closed my eyes. Because of this, I was able to move away from fretting about lunch and the afternoon, able to move away from *myself* as the center of the experience and let myself be drawn to and reconnected with the world outside. In that unity I discovered myself surrendering to the presence of God.

The pattern of my surrendering to the sounds at noon has elements that sometimes predominate in contemplative prayer:

1. Being open to the experience.
2. Being drawn out of oneself.
3. Noticing the distinctions in what is being contemplated.
4. "Staying with" what has been noticed as one would sit quietly with a companion.
5. Letting feelings in the heart emerge.
6. Expressing oneself out of those feelings to God.
7. Being open to response.

Watching a beautiful sunset; noticing the variations of the autumn leaves; sitting with the sun on the first spring day—contemplation is a familiar experience. Because we have all had our contemplative moments and found them fruit-bearing, if I suggest that remembering Jesus in a contemplative way can be an approach to prayer that bears fruit, it should come as no surprise. To suggest that Jesus approached life contemplatively may be a bit surprising to some readers, however, for some believers perceive Jesus as always being remarkably involved and busy.

Jesus and Contemplation

The choices from the gospels to illustrate this are abundant. I will begin with two that have some commonality.

Open to the culture in which he lived, Jesus did not seem to approach it by pre-judging people. On the other hand, he did seem to notice particularly those folks others overlooked or rejected, like children, tax collectors, and widows.

One day, with a great number of people and disciples around him, he approached the gate of the town of Naim and paused to watch a burial procession for a young man who had been an only son. In spite of the "considerable number of townspeople" in the procession, Jesus noticed the widowed mother who would be twice bereft now, without a husband and a son. As he gazed at her, Jesus "felt sorry for her." Attending to her in her distress, Jesus told her not to cry. After raising the young man to life, Jesus, still aware of the grieving woman, "gave him to his mother" (Lk 7:11–17).

Later in Luke's gospel, we find Jesus noticing another widow. Standing in the courtyard of the temple, Jesus was watching people, primarily rich people, put their monetary offerings into the treasury. Jesus' attention is drawn to a poor widow. As she deposits her coin, Jesus seems to sense keenly the proportionality of her giving, and he remarks on the distinction between her and the others who have contributed. The widow has given more than any of the rich, he says, because "she from the little she had has put in all she had to live on" (Lk 21:1–4). Contemplating this widow, Jesus seems to lift her up from her poverty as he lifted up from death the son of the widow of Naim. A woman who might be overlooked because of her poverty or looked at only because of her poverty, Jesus contemplates because of her *generosity*. The widow giving her mite has become an example for all generations of what true giving really is.

Whether walking through cornfields, strolling on the shores of the Sea of Galilee, or passing through the gates of a town along the road, Jesus sustained a contemplative approach to life. *Open to the experience around him,* he seldom seems to rush, though he lived in an age when men and women traveled by foot, going no faster than three miles an hour. In spite of this, Jesus resisted the disciples' urge to hurry.

Jesus also seemed *to notice distinct elements* in what was going on, i.e., noticing, not the amounts, but the proportionality of those who contributed to the treasury, seeing in what he noticed distinctions in generosity.

Staying with the situation at hand, Jesus seemed to *let feelings emerge* in his heart such as pity for the widow of Naim.

In story after gospel story, in parable after parable that Jesus told, we sense his awareness of persons and life around him—the threshing of the grain, the drawing of water from a well. We discover that Jesus responded to what he saw—turning toward, not away, from a funeral procession, touching a leper who calls out to him. Contemplating Jesus, we realize that mission for him did not mean separation from the life around him. Instead of heedlessly rushing toward goals and accomplishments, Jesus let himself be drawn toward the life around him even when that disturbed others and caused them to question his motives. Noticing particular elements in that life around him, Jesus was free enough to let feelings come into his heart. Action then emerged—from a contemplative stance.

Contemplation and Ordinary Life

If contemplation was an everyday occurrence for Jesus, then contemplation is a dynamic calling for our attention as an approach to everyday life. When it's a missing ingredient *in that setting*, having it be an ingredient in prayer is more unlikely. Because we so often insist on traveling at a pace equivalent to the speed limit we set on our cars, we may not be as naturally contemplative as people who traveled at three miles an hour were. What that means is that we need to step back periodically and see the woods as well as the trees (as we are doing now). Doing this, we may discover that the way we approach life and ministry has its parallel in the way we approach prayer—if we rush through the activities of our life, we may rush through prayer. If we approach these activities as duties to be endured, we may bring that attitude to prayer and feel relief only when we cross prayer off our inventory of chores. To approach life, ministry, and prayer the way Jesus did—open to experience, noticing distinct elements, staying with these, letting feelings of the heart emerge, and finding in this unity God's presence—may call for some fundamental changes.

If there's a devil's advocate in the crowd, that person is now asking, "Do you know how hard it is to break ingrained habits?"

Changing one's pace from 55 miles an hour to even 35 miles an hour is no easy task, I admit. It calls for fine-tuned motivation and thoroughness in realizing one's destination. Because the destination of this chapter is developing contemplative awareness in regard to life and prayer, and because contemplation is elusive, we are examining it from all perspectives in order to get a good grasp on the way it functions. Examining ourselves and the way we function can also be fruit-bearing. It can help us to notice and name times in our own lives when we have approached life in a truly contemplative manner, enabling us to exercise this option more frequently and fully.

One problem in linking contemplation to everyday, ordinary life is that everyday, ordinary life easily becomes routine, causing our senses, and our skill at noticing, and, sadly, even our hearts, to become numb. Being numb is the arch-enemy of being contemplative.

Jesus was constantly on the road. Traveling from town to town, Jesus maintained a freshly contemplative approach to life. There may be more than coincidence at work here. On the road is seldom routine.

Journey and Ministry

Standing back and taking a look at journey is another way to deepen one's understanding of the contemplative approach. Most of us can't live as mobile a life as Jesus did but we can reflect on journeys we have taken and notice how they evoke a contemplative dynamic. A trip opens the door to new vistas, compelling us, whether we like it or not, to look at God's creation and to experience life beyond our routine. Sometimes, on a trip, we *savor* creation and the experiences we have, and sometimes we do not. Nonetheless, a journey cannot help but stimulate noticing and feeling.

For example, our twin daughters, Katherine and Pamela, graduated from college in California five years ago, and George, Tierney and I took our maiden voyage by car across the country to attend the graduation. Later, reflecting on this journey, I discovered that:

—we all contemplated some of the same experiences.

—each of us contemplated some experiences differently.

—each of us contemplated different aspects of some experiences.

Let me explain.

On departure, no one urged us to contemplate cows in Kansas. One of the mutual delights of our trip, however, was traveling across Kansas during a lingering sunset that silhouetted, here and there, a cow, darkened into shadow against a glowing horizon.

Later on the trip, George, Tierney, and Katherine, newly graduated, savored the Grand Canyon. The same cannot be said of me. One careful, cautious look into its depth and its breadth evoked an overwhelming awe and dread in me. The rest of our day at the canyon I spent shopping for groceries, washing clothes, writing postcards about the canyon's beauty, worrying about the part of the family that had descended into it, and finally arguing with God about the creation of a vista surely not intended for human eyes.

A third experience taught me how each of us contemplated different aspects of a mutual experience. Let's return for a moment to Kansas. The mellow feeling evoked by the cows at sunset ended abruptly when night descended, our left rear tire went flat, the jack refused to work, and no motorist on the heavily trafficked highway stopped to help us. Finally a car zoomed by carrying a boat. A boat in the heart of Kansas? The second surprise came when the boat and car stopped and the driver offered us a ride into Abilene.

The next morning, tire and jack fixed, we opened the motel's Gideon Bible to read a passage before departing for what we hoped would be a less demanding day. "Read the good Samaritan," George said. "I woke up thinking about that passage."

After the reading, we sat in silence for a moment; then I spoke, thanking God for the good Samaritan who had carried us as well as his boat into Abilene. When I finished, my husband said quietly, "I had forgotten him. To me the good Samaritans were the two guys from the garage who were willing to work past closing time to tow the car. Thanks for them, Lord."

Tierney spoke then, "Falling asleep last night, I thought of how *we* were good Samaritans—to one another I mean. When the car broke down and nobody stopped for so long, each of us tried to help each other—to be relaxed and hope and not be afraid. Let's thank God for that!"

Cows in Kansas, a mutually savored experience; the Grand Canyon, a selectively savored experience; good Samaritans, savoring different aspects of the same experience—what do these journey events teach us about contemplation, ministry and prayer?

If our pilgrim ship, the church, is on a journey with many passengers on board, then sometimes we passengers will mutually contemplate the same experience (for example, the reading of the Passion on Palm Sunday). Sometimes each of us in our diverse daily lives and ministries will contemplate and savor different experiences, and sometimes we will contemplate the same experience yet savor different aspects of it.

Different aspects of the same experience can be seen in the following examples.

Sam and Molly are both lectors. But for each it is a different journey of faith. As they prepare regularly for carrying out ministry, they both feel drawn to delve more deeply into Scripture. Sam is discovering that he is intrigued by the stories of the Old Testament; on the other hand, Molly is attracted to the spiritual depth in St. Paul's epistles.

Betty and Bill are both eucharistic ministers. But for each it is a different ministerial journey. For Betty, the high point of her ministry is bringing Communion to patients at a nearby hospital; she is moved by the fidelity to God she finds in those who are suffering. For Bill, distributing the Communion bread during Sunday liturgy is the high point of his ministry; he is moved by the solemnity and reverence he notices in the eyes of his fellow parishioners as they approach the altar. During the week, Betty contemplates the patients in the hospital and engages in petitionary prayer for them. Bill often finds himself contemplating the faces of those whom he has served as a eucharistic minister, and his heart is moved to feelings of gratitude for the spiritual community he senses in his parish.

There is no right or wrong, no good, better, best, in all of this—just as in my story about the good Samaritans, neither Sam or Molly, Betty or Bill is more right about what is *spiritually* evoked by their ministry.

What is savored needs no measure; contemplative *variations* weave the tapestry of faith we identify as community.

Discovering one's own particular contemplative approach to one's ministry saves the ministry from becoming only a task accomplished for the church week after week. It easily and naturally unfolds into prayer.

Becoming contemplative overnight about one's everyday life is a tall order. Because *ministry* may be a new venture, one that has *not yet become routine,* it can provide a unique opportunity for embarking on the contemplative approach to prayer. During the initial experiences of ministry, people often feel awkward. Self-conscious about being "showy," they may feel that their spiritual side, a part of them that has always been somewhat hidden, is on parade much as a finger would be if it were in a splinter wrapped in adhesive tape. Just as one would want that finger, in appearance, to become again a natural part of the body, one feels more comfortable when one's participation in a particular ministry is integrated into one's ongoing faith life.

"Is that possible? Can I integrate my ministry into my regular faith life or has my ministry changed my faith?" you may ask yourself.

For followers of Jesus, faith open to change is essential. But integration is also essential even if one's faith is changing. A faith life that is compartmentalized, with some compartments not on speaking terms with others, becomes a burden one must shoulder, not a spiritual foundation that supports and sustains daily life.

On the other hand, *ministry* not only brings new experiences into one's life, it also evokes a religious ambiance. This ambiance and this freshness breaks the ordinary routine into which even our faith can sometimes slump. Because of this, ministry is not only a challenge needing integration, it is an *opportunity that can energize* our ongoing faith with vitality, and help us perceive the people and happenings in our everyday life more contemplatively.

In a sense that is what this book is all about. And in this chapter we have considered so far two approaches in regard to ministry and one's spiritual life. The first is considering *contemplation as a fruitful approach* to life, to ministry, and to God in prayer. The second consideration is *reflecting on journey* as a dynamic that easily evokes contemplative experiences, illustrated by Jesus' life and by my story about the trip to California. The fruit of this, I hope, is a perception of ministry as *journey rather than function.*

Journey and Spiritual Life

Perceiving faith and ministry as journey is the key to the integration of ministry, prayer and spirituality. Expanding our notion of journey enables this.

One night, while watching television, I wondered if we always have to go away to embark on a journey. George, Pam and I were watching a National Geographic program about the rain forest in Costa Rica. At first I busied myself with something else whenever insects were on the screen. Pam did the same whenever snakes appeared. Before long, however, the rain forest became so engrossing that our hesitations evaporated, and we were, as the saying goes, glued to the screen by its fascinating beauty. Our curiosity was so engaged that it seemed as if we were right there in the rain forest.

I tell this story to illustrate that sometimes it is possible to see beyond a particular locale and even to scale barriers like distaste for insects and snakes and sense oneself as a participant in what is *not* everyday and ordinary.

Among the Christians I know, there are some who seem to grasp the fact day after day after day that they are on a journey with God. And they realize that this journey is *not* everyday and ordinary in spite of routine, and in spite of fears, and in spite of insects and snakes on the road that could cause them to turn away from that journey.

Most of us are more timid and tepid. We fear that if we make too much of our journey with God we will abandon our routine duties or, conversely, that we will have to perfect the routine. Or we grow petulant, disclaiming the journey and Jesus' personal role in our lives because, in the midst and turmoil of life, the turmoil is technicolor and Jesus and the journey are in black and white. We want the turmoil in sepia tones, and Jesus in technicolor—and the kingdom of heaven by next Friday please!

If journey with God continually has a primary place in one's consciousness, what seems routine in everyday life is no longer always routine. This not only reinforces the sense of journey in one's consciousness, it is part of the provision *for* the journey with God. Events in ordinary life become fresh; experienced with the Spirit, they become events that evoke feeling just as the cows in Kansas and the Grand Canyon did for me and my family on our trip. Friends, neighbors—yes, even relatives—at times are seen as good Samaritans when life is contemplated as a journey with God.

Both ministry and a contemplative approach to life are significant here. Approached contemplatively, one's ministry becomes an opportunity for a special journey into one's faith where one can experience God more deeply. This happens more readily, of course, if one perceives ministry as *part* of one's faith and not vice versa, i.e., that doing one's ministry takes care of one's faith journey for the week.

In addition, one becomes open to *all* the resources available to develop one's spiritual life. It is amazing how stingy we can sometimes be about the ingredients we are willing to use in the recipe for a better faith life. Here is where the role of contemplation comes in again, for the more contemplative we are, the more expansive we are about the means to increase our faith.

Memory and Imagination

Two ingredients that are often overlooked, ingredients that are essential to developing a contemplative approach, are memory and imagination.

Sometimes *remembering* an event or a person and savoring that memory can lead us into a tangible awareness of God, as the following story illustrates:

During a particularly painful and lonely time a few years ago, a time when ministry was hard and prayer was arid for me, I traveled across the state to worship with the people of The Vineyard. At the coffee hour following the Mass, a lay minister friend crossed the crowded room, stood beside me, and said quietly, "This fall you kept coming into my mind. I don't know if you were having troubles or not, but each time I saw you, I prayed for you. I just wanted you to know." She touched my hand gently and then moved into conversation about another topic.

That simple confession and gesture came back to me on the long drive home. As I remembered her words and gesture, I was struck by the fact that though I could not reach out to others in September and October, another person, not even knowing my troubles, had been sensitive enough to carry me before God in prayer when I came into her mind. As I savored my own memory of our short encounter at the coffee hour, I saw the concern in her eyes for me. I felt the touch of her hand. Gradually, my tight grip on the steering wheel eased, my shoulders moved out of the brace weeks of stress had formed around them, and I murmured, "Thank you, Jesus"—my first *spontaneously* articulated prayer of the fall season.

My friend had been, of course, an encounter with love from God. Remembering led to my feeling healed.

Imagination is another resource for prayer that needs dusting off. We humans are sometimes suspicious of our power to imagine and confused about whether it belongs in the vice or virtue bin. People are often startled when I suggest that God can come to them through their imaginations as well as through their sense of hearing, seeing, touching, feeling, and remembering.

Here is an instance of how a group used imagination to deepen prayer. After a winter series of parish talks on the bishops' pastoral on war and peace, men and women involved in the parish's social justice ministry decided to meet weekly during the spring to pray for peace before discerning appropriate actions.

At the first gathering, Nora said, "As far back as I can remember, I have been praying for peace. When I was in the sixth grade and buying defense stamps and waiting in line for rationed butter, I prayed World War II would end and peace would come. The Korean war and the war in Vietnam and today the troubles and terrorists in the Middle East and in Northern Ireland as well as the agonies in Central America prod me to continue to cry out, 'Lord, help us make the world peaceful!' Now it's the nuclear arms race that frightens me the most and makes me petition all the more for peace." The prayer for peace shared at that gathering and the next resembled Nora's prayer, "Lord, help us make the world peaceful!" Very soon the gatherings felt repetitive and tiresome.

For Lent the group decided to adopt a different approach.

Borrowing an idea from the grocery shelf, "Wednesday is Prince Spaghetti Day," the peace ministry group made Wednesday, their meeting day, the Prince of Peace Day.

Each Wednesday, for a brief while, tapes of calming, quiet music would be played. Sitting with the Spirit as their companion, the lay ministers asked God to encourage their imaginations in order to sense the world at peace. Sometimes one would imagine armaments being collected and thrown into the sea, another would imagine the troubled places of the world without death and conflict, and a third would imagine our own land without violence in the cities, with injustice vanishing and white and black living in harmony, particularly where suburban wealth now excludes the latter. As they shared their visions and prayed together they sensed their fervor and desire for peace intensifying. Before long each member of the social justice ministry as well as the group as a whole became active in projects related to arms reduction and peace.

Before moving on, it might be helpful to see how Eileen, a lay woman engaged in the ministry of home visitation, utilized memory and imagination in her contemplative approach to ministry and prayer. Oftentimes, after a visit to a shut-in elderly person in her parish, Eileen would take a few moments in the evening to pray. At first her prayers were very wordy and inclusive of all the elderly she knew. After a while she began to bring into her prayer only the person she had visited that day, and Eileen would let the memory of that visit flow through her senses. One evening when she was contemplating Mrs. Palfrey, she heard the woman say again, as she had early that morning, "You know, Eileen, you're church for me. Without you I wouldn't have any connection with church anymore." Eileen had felt awed when Mrs. Palfrey whispered the words to her, and in prayer, remembering that moment, Eileen's eyes filled with tears and she felt as if God were placing a blanket of love on her shoulders.

When visiting Mrs. Palfrey, Eileen was sometimes asked to massage the elderly woman's arms and legs with lotion. Often, while doing this, Eileen had a strong sense that Jesus was present as promised in Matthew 25, living in those who are weak and needy.

Praying with immediate memories, Eileen found that she was not as restless in prayer and that her prayer seemed to have more depth. Some evenings Eileen imagined Mr. Owens and Mrs. Palfrey, the two parishioners she visited most frequently, as they might have been when they were young or as they will be when God brings them to live with him forever. During these prayers, Eileen often felt and expressed gratitude for knowing each of the persons to whom she was ministering. Through these prayers of imagination, she found that she went forward in her ministry with more hope in her heart. And she was able to reveal more affection on her visits.

Eileen, it is obvious, by using a contemplative approach to prayer and by using all the resources for prayer available to her, deepened not only her prayer but also her understanding of her spiritual journey by being open to the Spirit, improvising within her heart.

Most believers, especially those who minister in the name of Jesus, want to experience more depth in prayer. What is apt to be overlooked is the significance of preparation, of readying the soil and planting the seeds. In this chapter, certain elements have been highlighted, elements that contribute to the process of prayer:

—responding to the impulse to pray with the heart, not the head, which means not forcing or controlling the prayer but being open to the experience, to the Spirit and to the feelings that emerge within.

—approaching life contemplatively as Jesus did to avoid the numbness routine can evoke.

—developing awareness that ministry is a journey within one's faith and that life is a journey with God we call faith.

—using memory and imagination as resources for prayer that emerges with ministry.

—noticing and savoring particular moments of ministry with God.

Savoring

Fr. Walter Burghardt, S.J. calls contemplation a long, loving look at the real. Savoring is a word that has cropped up in our text not by accident, for when we take a long loving look at the real, sometimes we savor what we sense is real. Savoring is an activity universally experienced. Fresh spring asparagus, the first crop of corn on the cob, new Macintosh apples in the fall—the list of foods that people savor is endless. Savoring is as common as falling in love, and when we do fall in love, what is more natural than contemplating in a savoring way the one we love.

This familiar dynamic is at the heart of contemplative prayer. Whether your contemplative approach is memory, imagination, or openness to the experience at hand, you are drawn beyond the narrowness of "me" and led sometimes to the ultimate prayer, savoring God.

The easiest way to begin praying contemplatively is to start your prayer by remembering what you savor, sitting with that and sharing the delight with the Lord. Another way to begin is to let prayer emerge within an activity, such as listening to music or walking in the woods, an activity that you find natural in establishing a contemplative mood.

Also helpful is becoming attracted to what Jesus savored. By noticing his relish for children, his eagerness to heal a blind man, the depth of his appreciation for the woman who anointed him at Bethany, we are encouraged to respond to those to whom we minister with our hearts and not just with techniques managed by our heads. Putting his affectivity on the reserve shelf to be taken out only on occasion was never Jesus' habit, though it, unfortunately, became a habit that infiltrated Christian tradition. Only a heart open to whatever experience in life emerges, a heart ready with affectivity, can savor strangers and friends and call them to be close as kin.

As ministers of the Lord, we may be intrigued to discover how much Jesus cherished those who ministered in his time. In Luke's gospel, in chapter ten, the disciples return to Jesus rejoicing in the effectiveness of their ministry. Jesus says, "I watched Satan fall like lightning from heaven. Yes, I have given you power to tread underfoot serpents and scorpions and the whole strength of the enemy; nothing shall ever hurt you."

His elation is boundless but he points to what *they should savor* in regard to their ministry—not their accomplishments but the grace bestowed by the Father: "Yet do not rejoice that the spirits submit to you; rejoice rather that your names are written in heaven."

As the passage continues we see and hear Jesus, uplifted with joy by the Holy Spirit, move within the experience of savoring his disciples to a savoring of the Father whom he cherishes as "Lord of heaven and earth": "I bless you, Father, Lord of heaven and earth, for hiding these things from the learned and the clever and revealing them to mere children. Yes, Father, for that is what it pleased you to do."

In these passages alone we have a remarkable guide to prayer for our ministries. No false modesty should prevent us from savoring those special moments and times in ministry when our faith touches another, when healing seems to be the grace enabled, when a child shares a faith-filled insight, or when gratitude is the response to hospitality we have extended.

These are the moments to bring to prayer and savor with Jesus as the early disciples did, letting him move your heart into cherishing God, the One who enables all ministry which bears fruit.

Lingering in the Shadows

Life, including ministry, on the other hand, sometimes confronts us with pain. Elation, we are reminded in the Book of Proverbs, is not always appropriate:

It is to treat a wound with vinegar,
To sing songs to a sorrowing heart (Prv 25:20).

Life is sometimes strewn with sorrowful mysteries. In addition to our own personal hurts, we may encounter in our own lives and in the lives of those we know, not only tragic events, but also the darkness and despair that these can evoke.

Is there a place for contemplation in all of this? Can our response be both prayerful and honest?

One of the elements of contemplation mentioned earlier was *staying with* what emerges without forcing control on it. Savoring, one approach to staying with, is complemented by what I call *lingering in the shadows.*

This can be difficult to do. In our culture and in this century, adults have lost the child's gift of articulating hurts spontaneously. The gift of trust has become fractured, the trust a child has that someone will listen to his or her hurts and respond with gestures of love. To linger in the shadows, to stay with feelings that are somber or painful *and* share them with others and with God, can seem embarrassing or burdensome. In ministry, not only those to whom we minister, but often we ourselves hide the hurt in the heart, even from our own eyes. The danger in flight is that the attention we pay to persons as we minister can begin to flit from surface to surface as if we were darning needles called to skirt the surface of life and faith.

By encouraging savoring it is not my intention to suggest a denial of the very real and harsh feelings we experience in life. The healthiest and holiest persons I have known seem to be men and women who have the freedom and maturity to experience a *range of feelings.* We lose sight of an important path to prayer, and we diminish our agility to facilitate depth if we feel we must dress our feelings in their Sunday best before revealing them to others or to God.

Indeed, our unwillingness to linger in the shadows can have sad consequences for us. Because we dare not stay with our hearts when they are bruised, not only do we lessen our ability to help others, but our own hearts are never wholly healed by the Spirit. Consequently, when a fresh hurt comes our way, it activates the buried hurts that remain unhealed below the surface.

Lingering in the shadows with God, whom we perceive as a companion and not as a magician who takes all pain away, can often enable us to move through dark feelings, become free of them, and savor the ordinary and the sublime again.

The promise of the gospel is that Jesus will be with the sorrowing heart. We who are his ministers are not only called to imitate him in this but also to imitate his willingness to reveal the sorrow in his own heart. Jesus had the courage to stay with his feelings of sorrow. We sense a maturity in his weeping over Jerusalem, a poignancy in his sorrow for the people because they were harassed and dejected. Though he cut no corners in describing the rigors of the apostolic life, he was able to contemplate it and himself compassionately. We sense this especially in sayings like, "Foxes have holes and birds of the air have nests, but the Son of Man has nowhere to lay his head."

At Gesthemene we discover the most contemplative prayer in existence. In El Greco's painting of this scene the profundity of the prayer is revealed—sorrow affects the garment Jesus wears, painted in blood tones of rose and red, and the landscape surrounding him as though his anguish was an awesome tremor passing through the earth. Sorrowful unto death, Jesus turns to his friends but they sleep. Sorrowful unto death, he turns again to the Father and lingers in the shadow death has already cast.

Agony is not meant to be shared only with oneself; isolation is the path on which despair lies waiting. Compassion for self, the consolation of Jesus, the companionship of others—each is a Christian response to suffering. When my heart seems hurt beyond repair, I sit in stillness with the cross. Staying with what Jesus endured for all humankind allows me to let go of the brokenness of my heart, letting it flow into the beatenness of his body. That process enables me to share my sorrow with others.

And Jesus from the cross invites this kind of sharing by initiating the ministry of bereavement when he entrusts his mother into the hands and heart of his beloved disciple John, and entrusts John into the hands and heart of his mother.

Lay men and women today who have the courage and compassion called for in the hospice ministry and the ministry of bereavement continually live out in their ministries the spirit of Jesus when he as he was dying, initiated a new ministry by bonding his friend and his mother, two who loved him as he loved them. "Son, behold your mother." "Mother, behold your son."

When we discover that sorrow is sometimes the most appropriate response to life, our faith lives deepen because we have learned to say "no" to two negative alternatives: despair and destructive disregard for self.

Trusting that God is with us in the shadows is the cornerstone for that discovery.

In this chapter we have been reflecting on our lives, for our lives include our spirituality, faith, ministry and prayer. Sometimes these facets of our lives can become strangers to one another. A contemplative approach is often suggested because a gift of contemplation is the integration of activity with spirituality. Ministry and prayer, faith and ordinary activities converge into unity when life is approached contemplatively.

Workaholism and stress, health problems and cardinal sins of our culture, subvert time for prayer; they also crush a disposition that invites *awareness of* the *persons* encountered in life and an *awareness of* the *experiences* we live day by day. Both lingering with those who touch the heart and savoring those who catch particular sensibilities within us deepen our awareness of God. When we live aware of the life we actually live, we find ourselves at times *absorbed* by a variety of realities—the sounds at noon, cows in Kansas, Jesus in the gospels, peace on earth, people's faces as they come to Communion, the sick, the old, the dying. When this happens the heart is often compelled to *articulate itself to God.*

Awareness, absorption, and *articulation* form a delicate balance that often determines the quality of our prayer and ministry. Although talking to God is sometimes perceived as equivalent to prayer, perpetual "talkiness" can impede dialogue and so favor the articulation dynamic that awe, reverence, and absorption become minimal. One is actually talking to self more than to God.

Never to address the Giver in appreciation for the gifts given is the situation at the other extreme. If one savors or lingers in the shadows yet never speaks directly to God within the experience, one is probably being untrue to his or her nature in the way that it functions in everyday life. To articulate, to compliment and show gratitude, dresses our ordinary existence and is an essential dynamic of our human self in which our spiritual self is rooted. Most Americans are not handicapped in articulating what they *think;* difficulties sometimes emerge, however, from an inability to articulate what they *feel.*

Finding one's way back to the heart, affirming the feelings of the heart, sharing them with God—this is the road to be taken if one wants to minister and to realize one's spiritual identity and destiny.

10

WATERING, WEEDING, WATCHING DEVELOPMENTS

Contemplation is the French intensive way to pray. Let me explain with a story.

Leslie and Jeff, my oldest daughter and her husband, have a garden behind the small, yellow house where they live between hillsides dotted with cows in Vermont. Since Jeff's folks live in farm country in Pennsylvania, Jeff takes snapshots from spring planting to fall harvesting so that his mother and dad can compare growth in their garden with his. Those of us from Massachusetts pitch in with watering and weeding on midsummer visits.

Leslie has learned a lot since she was their daughter Nicole's age and greeted me one afternoon with a bunch of posies: "Pretty flowers, Momma." She smiled as she handed me all the blossoms from our dozen tomato plants. She and Jeff credit French intensive farming for their bounty. This method calls for shoring up the earth in spring, so the seeds and infant plants are placed in waist high soil with deep troughs between the rows.

Late one afternoon, picking tomatoes and eggplants and peppers and beans and corn for supper, Leslie and I talked about all the components of their way of gardening. Studying the seed catalogues in winter, tending to tiny seedlings in spring, ordering the truckload of manure that was the gift from wife to husband for husband's April birthday, watering, weeding, pruning—all are credited along with shaping the land and forming the soil for the bounty harvested in the fall.

This chapter's extended introduction is by way of suggesting that reaping harvests in ministerial and prayer life calls for similar attention to detail and cultivation of soil—even to letting the grass grow tall around the garden, i.e., letting go of rival activities to find time for prayer.

The last chapter was a consideration of events and encounters, some ministerial, all approached contemplatively, that unfolded into prayer. The instances cited were as varied as life itself:

—the sounds at noon;

—a flat tire;

—the Grand Canyon;

—eucharistic ministry;

—the disciples returning from ministry to Jesus;

—visits to the elderly;

—a confrontation with death.

What has not yet been considered were all the details like environment that encourage or discourage prayer.

When asked what one should pray about, a rabbi many years ago said: "Anyone who has eyes to see and ears to hear will find each day a hundred opportunities to give blessings to God."

What a delightful sentiment—and easy to activate when one is near the hillsides and gardens of Vermont. Some of us, however, are not in situations that the rabbi's remark suggests, and some of us lack antennae as contemplatively sensitive as his. To take advantage of those encounters and events that *do* touch our heartstrings, we water the soil with what is familiarly called "regular" prayer—the loaf and fish that upon occasion becomes super-abundance. The conviction sustaining this sentiment is that it is by coming to the Lord day by day that spiritual development eventually will be there to be watched.

Finding My Spot

As I write this I am in another pastoral setting. I am watching fishermen in a lobster boat search for the *sea's* bounty in traps previously set here in the Atlantic Ocean by the Eastern Point Retreat House in Gloucester, on the North Shore of Boston. Where I sit has been worn into a seat by hundreds of retreatants who pray in nooks and crannies hidden in the glorious outcropping of rock created millenniums ago by volcano and earthquake. For years, women and men, including myself, have experienced serenity and joy, tears of sorrow and gladness, and intimate outpourings of heartfelt love while praying in the niches formed in this cathedral of stone, blessed by spray of the sea.

"I found my spot." On the second or third day of an eight day retreat, a retreat director is apt to hear that from more than one retreatant. And sometimes the spot indicated is not a crevice by the ocean; it may be by the hollyhocks in the Mary Garden or by the pond at the end of the drive. Or it may be in the simplicity of one's small bedroom that looks out at the sea or in at the woods. One thing is certain: "finding my spot" has something to do with the quality of one's prayer. Until one finds one's spot a restlessness can be pervasive within the one trying to pray. As David Fleming, S.J. says, paraphrasing St. Ignatius, "Sometimes what appears to be an action or event of small consequence can affect the course of prayer for a whole day or a number of days."[1]

The reference is applicable to home where *finding my spot* can be ten times more difficult than here at the retreat house.

When Setting Is at Home—Some Preliminaries

When I was a little girl, daily prayer was a relatively easy matter. On my way home from school, I stopped to make a visit. I said the stations or lit a candle at Mary's altar in the church around the corner. But what do we do today when the church around the corner is locked except for services or is not around the corner, demanding a trip by car or bus?

The desire to initiate a daily time for prayer demands of us a search for a spot where prayer will be evoked as it was in that church around the corner. A rule of thumb for setting: don't give up the search for a suitable spot even if a half dozen are tried and found wanting. The closet to which Jesus invites you may more easily be found in a convent than in a duplex bursting at the seams with a dozen assorted kids, dogs, televisions, and radios. But a prayer place perfect for you can be found!

For me it's beside the stereo. On with the earphones. On with one of my favorite instrumental records. Down with the lids of my eyes. Out—tuned out completely: voices, television, telephone, temptation to give up trying to pray.

At first the family may react. Shake your arm. Gesture for you to remove the earphones. Say, "I'm awfully sorry if I disturbed your prayer coming into the room, Dad." Or, "Ma, are you prayin' again?" They all learned to tie their shoes and spell their names. They will learn to leave you alone if you, interiorly, can leave them alone while you are attempting to pray.

What is remarkable about our day and age in regard to prayer is not that prayer was forsaken when "make a visit" went out of style but that believers have found a variety of settings in which to encounter God in a focused way. With little effort, six Christians immediately come to mind who engage in prayer in a regular fashion in the following settings:

—in a nook in the pantry by a window;

—on a screened porch until the snow flies;

—walking tree-lined streets to the office;

—on a daily subway ride;

—in the living room with a candle when the family has gone to bed;

—while swimming laps in an indoor public pool.

"To each her own" was my response to the last setting on the list, but "to each her (or his) own" must, in a sense, *be* the motto for all. There is, after all, only one criterion—*here* is where I find the presence of God.

Last Sunday my youngest daughter Tierney, a drama major at New York University, and I gave a presentation on prayer to two hundred junior high and high school students at a parish in the diocese. At one point Tierney shared what she knows now as a college senior about prayer that she wished she had known in high school: "When we leave high schools and home towns, prayer doesn't just happen. We have to help make it happen. In New York City, I live on the fifteenth floor and work on the thirty-fourth floor. It was hard enough finding out how to live that way, but it was even harder searching out how to pray in my new settings in order to be *able* to live that way! Finding places to pray and finding out how to live in those places go hand in hand."

Whether in a penthouse or a pool, on a subway or a bench, when each of us has managed to "find my spot," there are other preliminaries to consider.

Inviting, Expecting, Listening—Watering the Soil

If we want to visit with a friend, we extend an invitation to meet for coffee or to walk along the river. If the invitation is accepted, we let our hearts anticipate the encounter, and that, in one way or another, readies us—paves the way—for a dialogue that eventually enhances the relationship.

Invitations from God are bountiful in Scripture, and we can mirror this on our side too, letting God know how deep our own desire for encounter is. If we are as expectant in mood for prayer as we are for meeting a friend, our anticipation readies the heart to listen as well as to speak. Because we know that God cares and God wants us to be honest, our time at prayer can be a time of venting frustrations about family, work, ministry or the globe in general.

God welcomes that, for God welcomes whatever is real within us. Occasionally, however, folks find themselves "drowning" in what they are sharing. Drained by the time it finally peters out, they make an exit from prayer without feeling the presence of God and, consequently, without waiting for God's response.

"If God doesn't use words to reply to me, how can I tell what God's response is even if I *do* listen?" This question is often asked by those discouraged by the listening component of prayer. Perhaps the expectation level within the minister coming to prayer is too high—or too low. Believers are often relieved when they discover that most people who pray do not receive a direct verbal response from God, e.g., the Lord addressing them in words. Signs of the Spirit's response vary but are seldom of the sort Moses experienced at the burning bush! Those most commonly indicated are:

—a change of mood—feeling peace where there was anxiety, sadness where there was fear, love where there was loneliness, anger where there was depression.

—a change of perception about proportionality—realizing a problem is surmountable—realizing other things have value beyond the disappointment expressed to God—realizing God will help you remove the sliver embedded in your heart.

—sensing an "answer" or an unexpected insight.

—seeing an image that sums up the reality better than words can express.

Distractions and Aridity—Weeds and Drought

Peter had a problem with prayer. In the synoptic gospels Peter is portrayed as a man more comfortable with spontaneously springing to action and with projections and promises about the future than he is with prayer. Even the privilege of being along with John and James on the mountaintop, when Jesus experiences prayer of such depth that it transfigures him and "his face shone like the sun," at first confers little more than enthusiasm on Peter who seems unable to surrender to the mystical dynamic of the experience as Jesus does.

Like many of us who pray, Peter seemed to enjoy the "golden glow" that prayer sometimes exhibits—"It is wonderful for us to be here"—but is easily distracted from it. Like Martha, after an initial encounter Peter becomes agitated by ambition and busy with building schemes: "I will make three tents here—one for . . . Moses . . . one for . . ."

Peter is probably the patron saint of those who fall prey to *distractions* in prayer. And how easy it is to follow Peter's footsteps, to turn off the experience before it has hardly begun, to take the first wave of response from God or the first insight and run away into the land of making plans or promises or shopping lists or solutions to problems. This "weed," unfortunately, represents only one form that distraction takes in prayer. But, using a pattern introduced in the last chapter, let's look at it. We can speculate about what may be happening within Peter who seems (a) unable to lose *awareness* of himself ("wonderful for *us* to be here", "*I* will build"); (b) unable to surrender to the experience and let himself be *absorbed* into it (as it moves on, Peter becomes fearful); (c) unable to *articulate* beyond a superficial and practical level.

Jesus, on the other hand, seems to free himself of self-awareness, to become fully absorbed by the experience, and to articulate its meaning only after they leave the mountaintop. He links the prayer to mission, for he relates "the vision" to the impending suffering in Jerusalem ("Tell no one about the vision until the Son of Man has risen from the dead"—Mt 17:1-13). In contrast, Peter's desire in the prayer experience seems shabby and shopworn: to contain an experience and cling to it by building tents for it—an expectation about experience that can never be fulfilled. Experiences always end.

The lesson in all of this for ridding oneself of the weeds of distractions? Perhaps it's to ask a hard question or two.

Am I coming to prayer to "kill two birds with one stone"? Oh, yes, to come closer to God but also to find peace because life is so tumultuous. Oh, yes, to put my relationship with God in first place, but also to find some answers to problems I encounter. Oh, yes, to deepen my love for the Lord but also to become a better minister.

Each "but also" encourages the center of prayer to be awareness of *self, not God,* absorption in *self, not God,* and articulation of *self* over against listening to *God*—in other words, being very human which may also mean being plagued by distractions.

Elbow grease is essential for digging up weeds, and elbow grease can be helpful in digging up distractions. What is not to be underestimated is focus.

Focus

If I come to pray to review, in a vague fashion, the whole day, my whole time at prayer can slither and slide from one incident to another, no incident anchored to a moment of depth. If I come with a focus and sit contemplatively, open to the experience and staying with the feelings that emerge, I may lose self-awareness, become absorbed in the experience, and feel my heart and God in mutual articulation.

Faith Journey as Focus

One focus for prayer that believers have found fruitful is their faith journey. In addition, spending time in prayer with this focus often reinforces one's faith which aids the prayer process. For example, remembering an experience of which you can say with certainty "God was there for me" and contemplating the encounter again in prayer lets memory move in as an *assisting* dynamic within the prayer.

In a similar vein, asking oneself "Who evangelized me?" and letting that person emerge in one's consciousness, then staying contemplatively with that person with God, can quicken one's appreciation for the initiation of the journey of faith and for the realization that evangelization preceded ministry.

Contemplating my grandfather is an instance of this from my prayer. Because my grandfather spoke only French and I spoke only English, we never were able to communicate with one another. As I matured I realized that, in spite of this impediment, my grandfather had spoken a powerful word of faith to me. One year he lived with my family. Each day except Sunday during that year, my grandfather walked to the church around the corner early in the morning and stayed there until late afternoon. Often I would make a visit and gaze at my grandfather; he would gaze back; neither of us would give a sign of recognition. Then I would go about my business—lighting a candle or saying the stations. Each time I left the church while he was there I felt a sense of wonder that anyone could love God so deeply and so faithfully that he would want to spend all day, every day, with God.

Without my knowing it, and probably without my grandfather knowing it, I was being evangelized.

The Ministerial Journey Within the Faith Journey as Focus

A second focus for prayer that others have found beneficial is one's ministerial journey within one's faith journey.

A minister engaged in spirituality in a large suburban parish, Sr. Judith, suggested this to Mark, who had been active in lay ministry for some time in various ways, yet who felt, in prayer, restless with distractions. Moments of doubt about the worth of his ministerial contribution also emerged. "Am I just going around in circles? That's what I'd really like to know," Mark exclaimed to Sr. Judith one evening before a meeting.

After tracing back with Mark the various ministries in which he had been involved, the nun suggested that he spend a week bringing each to the Lord and praying contemplatively with the memories that emerge. Mark had initiated his ministry as lector, and he was pleasantly surprised by the number of memories that came back from this ministry. While remembering an Easter when he had participated in several dramatic readings of the word for the vigil as well as a Mass when he had lectored and his youngest daughter had made her First Communion, Mark found himself savoring that ministry several times during his first week of trying this new approach to prayer.

When Mark was elected to the parish council, he ceased being a lector to give someone else in the parish a ministerial opportunity. The memories of parish council meetings that flooded his prayer the second week were not as consoling as those of the prior week. But, by the end of the week, Mark had a sense of his own gift for perseverance and of the Lord's appreciation for his ministerial leadership. After two terms on the council, Mark urged others to offer their very considerable gifts to the Lord in that ministry. Soon after the new election, Mark was invited to assist on the diocesan level with the Stewardship Appeal.

To stick with that focus in prayer for a week Mark found tedious. Although he appreciated the necessity of his labor on the Stewardship Appeal, the activity itself didn't "feel like ministry" to him. By the end of the week he was asking God to deepen his appreciation for those in the church who, as bookkeepers and business managers and financial consultants, serve in ways that others, and maybe themselves, seldom savor.

After the Appeal Drive, Mark was asked to serve on a diocesan task force on domestic violence. At this time Mark also approached the pastor, saying that he felt a strong desire to do "more heart-to-heart" ministry. The pastor suggested that Mark join classes preparing parishioners for the pastoral ministry of visiting parishioners who were chronically or terminally ill and in hospitals. In prayer the last week, Mark discovered that he had relished the classes more than the confrontation he found visiting patients to be. Surging up along with tears in his prayer were memories of the many times when he had felt helpless in the face of death and suffering and felt angry when abuse crippled children and the potential for happy childhood and mature adulthood. Midweek, anger at the pastor erupted in prayer when Mark blamed the pastor for suggesting that ministry to the sick was appropriate for Mark when "it was obvious," Mark told himself and God, "that I have no gifts or talents for that kind of service."

Mark was not prepared for these feelings or for the fact that the Lord did not seem to console Mark as he had in earlier prayer times. What Mark felt was a darker yet deeper sense of God with him, as a companion, within the tragedies and sorrows Mark found himself remembering. Toward the end of the week the cross emerged in his prayer, leading Mark to feel that the three years he had dedicated to hospital visitation ministry and to serving on the task force on domestic violence had been a time for him to know the cross as he had not known it personally before. As he later told Sr. Judith, "The month turned out to be like a mirror held up to help me see where I've grown spiritually. Putting me in the pulpit as a lector was like God feeding me pablum. The whole congregation, listening to you, is a lot simpler to minister to than trying to persuade Chuck Martin at the parish council meetings to listen to someone else besides himself. The council and the Stewardship Appeal seemed like God inviting me to stretch my capacities in different modes of ministry. To be honest, Sr. Judith, now I can admit that when I started ministry with the sick I thought that dropping by the hospital to cheer up the patients would put another feather in my church hat."

"And you found out?" Sr. Judith smiled.

"It damn near broke my heart. It showed me how little I had to give, but the leaders of the program, who have supervised me in the hospital, see that giving as effective. Lectoring, the parish council, the diocesan appeal—all are good, all challenged me to grow ministerially, but the hospital and the domestic violence task force dumped the cross in my lap. I heard the Lord say, 'Have you got the stuff to be true to me here, Mark?' Finally I had to face God and say, 'Without you I can't do these ministries because they break my heart!'"

Later Sr. Judith asked, "Are you still bothered by distractions?"

"What distractions?" Mark asked. Then he added, "You know, early on I was so enthusiastic about doing ministry in the church—I mean, right in St. James' church building. Praying about my ministries helped me see that the Lord had to lead me away from the building and into the world beyond the parish to show me what gutsy stuff ministry can really be!"

More on Uprooting Distractions

The weeds of distractions, which can grow wild and willful in contemplative prayer because the ambiance lacks structure, often wither when *focus* is brought to prayer, and when the one praying returns to the focus if stray thoughts or extraneous data make a foothold. For the person engaged in voluntary ministry on the parish level, a focus on faith journey or a focus on ministerial journey bears the additional fruit of helping the lay minister perceive the spiritual developments that faith and ministry have engendered.

Another way to approach distractions is to address God directly about one of the distractions. Persons of temperaments that don't easily settle into prayer often begin with a centering prayer and then move into contemplative prayer. A different twist, one that evokes a similar result, is engaging in reflection *before* going to prayer in order to sort out the priorities one wants to bring to God in prayer. Focus, however, differs from intentions that are petitionary and become litanies.

If one distraction persists over several prayer periods, that may very well be what your heart is longing to contemplate in prayer. Giving in to the urge that the distraction presents may lead to the left and the right hand, so to speak, discovering their mutuality. The hinge that often needs oiling is honesty within the heart.

Honesty, and courage about trusting that God will be hospitable to that honesty, is often the remedy for prayer that has become parched. Sometimes sharing the ins and outs of aridity with another person reveals the matter that is blocking the flow of feeling in prayer. The frustrations of drought may also be uprooted by going back in memory to vibrant times of prayer and engaging in a repetition of this prayer open to the Spirit.

Jumping Jacks—the Best Remedy for Distractions and Aridity

Earlier I referred to a program on prayer that my daughter Tierney and I presented for eighth, ninth, and tenth graders in a parish. We had prepared components of the program before that weekend. On the Sunday morning of the program we intended to work out the sequence of the components.

Because the house was in its typical Sunday morning uproar, to discern the order of the presentation we had breakfast in a nearby coffee shop. As I explained what I felt was a workable sequence, Tierney concentrated on her breakfast. Finally I said, "What do you think?"

Saturating her last piece of french toast with syrup, she was direct as she answered my question: "I am appalled!"

As I watched the syrup, drop by drop, fall back onto her plate she explained: "First these kids get herded in . . . then they get plunked down . . . then they get immediately talked *at* by . . . by . . . I hate to say this, Mom." Her eyes were sincere. "By someone these teenagers will connect with their mothers yakking at them. Or their teachers. Or even maybe their grandmothers!"

During the last remark her attention returned to that last piece of french toast.

"But I'm nowhere near old enough to be their grand mother!"

"We'll begin with Jumping Jacks!"

"Tierney, I didn't like the Jumping Jacks idea when you first suggested it. I can't think of anything worse to begin with."

"You've gotta trust, Mom. It works as a warm-up for acting; it'll work as a warm-up for prayer."

At the parish there was barely time to collect ourselves because Tierney, on seeing the church basement, was again appalled—this time at the 'choreography' of the chairs. A bit breathless from helping her turn two hundred chairs from rigid rows to concentric circles facing in another direction, I groaned as the two hundred, to my eyes somewhat self-conscious, seemingly reluctant if not resistant teenagers moved into the basement. They were barely in their seats when Tierney was up and on her toes in front of them, urging them up and out of their seats and into Jumping Jacks. Leaping high and clapping her hands over her head, she caught their fascination but not their cooperation.

"Where's the football captain?" Motioning with her arm, she cried, "Let's get him up here!"

When a dozen voices informed her that the football captain belonged to another church, she feigned horror, then drafted football, baseball, volleyball players and cheerleaders to center-stage where, pep-rally-style, they would invigorate everyone into attempting Jumping Jacks. There were no takers, but catcalls and kidding criss-crossed the room. Playful shoving and high-pitched giggles added to the disarray. My eyes traveled out the door, toward the parking lot where I wished my body could follow suit. Jolted by my daughter's voice sounding as though she wanted it heard across the high school football field, I came to.

"O.K., gang. Now we sit down! Now we move into some prayer! Now we meet the Lord through a contemplative guided meditation!" Turning to me with a beatific smile, she crooned, "*Now* they're all yours, Mom."

Creaking to my feet, I muttered to her, "Since the very beginning, I thought the Jumping Jacks idea was idiotic!"

To my surprise, when I invited the teenagers to close their eyes, most accepted the invitation. When I began to tell the story of Bartimaeus, the blind man who struggled to his feet and pushed through the crowd to find Jesus, most of the young people appeared to be listening. Tierney moved among them, then behind them, crying out as Bartimaeus did, "Son of David, have pity on me!" As I asked what Jesus asked Bartimaeus—"What do you want?"—many of the faces before me seemed absorbed in the experience we were sharing. As I invited them to hear Jesus ask *them* the question he asked Bartimaeus—"What do you want?"—I noticed how soft and glowing some of the faces had become.

We had been with these two hundred young persons less than fifteen minutes, yet they were already meeting Jesus in prayer.

I looked then at my daughter's face. Our eyes met. In that instant I knew I had much to learn about contemplation from her and her generation.

On the way home, I asked her if she was disappointed because so few in the group had done the Jumping Jack exercise.

"Not at all!" she replied. "The kidding and the shoving and the laughter relaxed them, robbed them of their self-conscious feelings and enabled them to flow with the guided meditation. That's what counts—getting out of their heads and into their hearts. And we did it, Mom!"

What also counted was that she had engaged them from the start; she had them "doing the scene" and helping to write the script as they did it. Even if I wasn't old enough to be their grandmother, I could never have done that. And that counts too.

Distractions mean one thing—limbo. Half in our heads, half in our hearts. Limbo—where we become like cars that keep stalling, going nowhere, but at the same time encouraging the driver to hate the car that's causing all the trouble.

There are times to be one hundred percent "in our heads." Prayer is not one of them. Whether it takes Jumping Jacks or jokes, come sometimes to the Lord "laid back." Then your agenda is apt to become absorption in your experience of the loving, challenging, indescribable God.

Praying Contemplatively with Scripture

Scripture is never a mere option for the Christian.

All ministers—those laboring in voluntary ministry, those engaged in professional ministry including vowed religious and ordained clergy, and those called to episcopal leadership—need to be nourished by the word, the word that teaches us that without Jesus there would be no ministry. Jesus called followers to discipleship; Jesus sent those formed by companionship with him into mission to minister throughout the world.

If the compass of the minister today is Jesus Christ, then contemplating Jesus in Scripture, contemplating the Scriptures that nourished Jesus, and contemplating the accounts of life in the earliest communities in Acts and the epistles is integral to the call of every Christian who ministers.

The ability to pray contemplatively with Scripture can be neither taken for granted by coordinators of voluntary ministry nor considered an after-thought to be slipped into the lay minister's back-pack when he or she is halfway through the ministerial journey. Learning how to pray with Scripture goes hand-in-hand with initiation into ministry.

Two helpful watchwords for the lay minister beginning to pray contemplatively with Scripture are *short* and *slow*. Passages in the synoptic gospels where Jesus encounters one other person often provide a beneficial focus that encourages dialogue if one contemplates the passage slowly.

Long passages as a personal stimulus for prayer easily become a quagmire. Because the complexities demand mental energy, the "head" rather than the "heart" is exercised. By-way after by-way encourages entanglement. The neophyte praying with Scripture by beginning with the three verses in the true relatives of Jesus passage (Lk 8:19-21) or the five verses of the Martha/Mary passage (Lk 10:38-42) may more easily move into a prayer of simplicity and depth than when praying with the forty-two verses of the woman at the well in John's gospel or the twenty-one verses in the conversation between Jesus and Nicodemus, also in John.

Men and women who frequently pray contemplatively with Scripture find that one or another of the following dynamics, during a particular prayer period, provides a catalyst for prayer that becomes encounter with God:

1. Staying with the same passage for several days.

2. Letting yourself be drawn to a word or phrase and savoring it.

3. Creating the scene described in the passage as fully as possible. Taking the time to visualize the details, hear the sounds, sense the mood. Seeing yourself in the scene speaking to Jesus, listening to Jesus.

4. Identifying with a person in the scene—Peter or Mary or the blind man. Sensing the feelings of that person as if they were your own.

5. Contemplating Jesus as he ministers. Seeing him, hearing him, sensing his feelings and spirit.

6. Letting the passage awaken memory and dwelling with it in an open way.

7. Asking the Lord to show you the passage as it would be lived in today's world.

Examples of how some of these dynamics were fruitfully applied may contribute to a tangible sense of contemplative prayer with Scripture. From my prayer journal, I have chosen excerpts related to the short passage in Luke on the healing of the leper:

Now Jesus was in one of the towns when a man appeared, covered with leprosy. Seeing Jesus he fell on his face and implored him. "Sir," he said, "if you want to, you can cure me." Jesus stretched out his hand, touched him and said, "Of course I want to! Be cured!" And the leprosy left him at once. He ordered him to tell no one. "But go and show yourself to the priest and make the offering for your healing as Moses prescribed it, as evidence for them" (Lk 5:12-14).

Before praying I also read the passage in Mark:

A leper came to him and pleaded on his knees: "If you want to," he said, "you can cure me." Feeling sorry for him, Jesus stretched out his hand and touched him. "Of course I want to!" he said. "Be cured!" And the leprosy left him at once and he was cured. Jesus immediately sent him away and sternly ordered him, "Mind you say nothing to anyone, but go and show yourself to the priest, and make the offering for your healing prescribed by Moses as evidence of your recovery." The man went away, but then started talking about it freely and telling the story everywhere, so that Jesus could no longer go openly into any town, but had to stay outside in places where nobody lived. Even so, people from all around would come to him (Mk 1:40-45).

Monday. After reading the passage through at a normal pace and then very slowly, sentence by sentence, I created the scene with my imagination, trusting that God can work through my imagination. I saw Jesus walking along a sandy road. His sandals kicked up dust on the road. The day seemed hot. He looked tired.

By the side of the road I sensed green foliage—at one point a good deal of it. Not palm trees—that surprised me. Tropical foliage with large, glistening, dark leaves.

Suddenly from behind a patch of foliage the leper stumbled toward Jesus. I didn't want to look at him. His coloring was the same as the dust in the road, his robe in tatters, his wrists and hands hidden in his robe. The face of the leper was hideous—pocked with craters. I wanted to look away. Then I heard him cry out to Jesus, "If you want to!" "If you want to!"

The leper fell at the feet of Jesus and started—begging? pleading? "If you want to!"

No one else Jesus would heal put it that way. "If you want to!" I felt that the man was groveling. Maybe he always groveled. I heard the cry again, and as I heard it I was struck by the lack of hope in it.

How tentative the leper was. Not demanding to be healed. Not enraged by his condition. Not, perhaps, even expecting to be healed. I sensed how often he had been pushed away—with words—because no one would even think of touching him. Brutal words, probably. I hear them. I see how children run from him, how mothers hide their babies from him. Not once but over and over and over he was told that he was an outcast, fit for nothing but the company of other lepers, all avoided as if they were a human dunghill.

"If you want to?" This time I hear the leper say more, say, "I know you don't want to. No one who isn't a leper would want to. No one has ever wanted to." Inside myself, I feel the darkness the leper feels, yet I also sense how magnetized he is by Jesus. Impelled to plead despite the hopeless feeling in his heart.

"If you want to." Within a memory is stirred of a time when I had begged as the leper was begging. And God had responded. Wordlessly I let the memory slip into God's hands.

Tuesday. Slowly I read the passage again and let the scene unfold in my imagination. I felt myself attracted to how Jesus initiated his ministry that day on that road.

"Of course I want to!" In my heart I centered on Jesus' words. "Of course I want to!"

As I stayed with Jesus' reply, I felt Jesus' sensitivity to the leper's deformed spirit as well as to his eroded body. Jesus spoke before he touched and healed the leper, yet what he said in speaking was part of the healing. I felt a gladness rise in me that Jesus had taken the time to assure the leper that what he wanted and what the leper wanted were *one and the same*—that in Jesus was the desire to respond to the leper's heart and soul as well as to his disfigured body. I sensed how moved Jesus was that the one who could have no human contact, except with other lepers, was trying to initiate contact on the human and personal level

of what *Jesus* desired as if the leper knew that Jesus' heart and
Jesus' power were meant to be aligned.

"Of course I want to!" I sensed that Jesus was touched
because the leper in the abyss of his loneliness had kept alive a
sensibility that the person was as important as the person's
body, so he cried, "*If* you want to." "If *you* want to."

"Of course I want to!" I felt awed by the urgency in Jesus'
heart, the urgency that the leper know, without a trace of mis-
giving, the strength of Jesus' desire that the leper be made whole.
Suddenly I found myself begging Jesus that in my ministry my
empathy could be as vibrant as his.

Wednesday. One image emerged after I spent a little time
again with the scene: Jesus lifting up the leper, then slowly drawing from the sleeves of the leper's garment the disfigured hands.
Holding them in his own cupped hands, he watched as they
slowly grew whole again. I stayed with the image for the entire
prayer time, feeling great gratitude.

Thursday. As I began to pray I remembered a story told to
me by a Jesuit friend who had led a retreat two years ago in a
leper colony in the Far East. There he met a remarkable man.
Most of the lepers seemed quite shy and more comfortable with
one another than with the Jesuit. But one man seemed more
confident, more like a leader than the others. This leper said that
the turning point for him came when the practice of taking Communion in the hand was introduced in the diocese. Sunday after
Sunday, the leper watched the nurses and doctors take the host
into their hands, but no leper, even those with several intact fingers, would take that step. As the weeks went on the struggle
within the man became a fierce tug of war between his strong
desires that he and the other lepers know God loved them
enough to let them take Communion in the hand, and his strong
fears that God would be angry if they let the body of his Son
touch their hands.

One Sunday the love for his people won out, and as he
approached the altar the leper extended his palms and the stubs
that had once been fingers. After the priest placed the host on
his palms the leper lifted them to his mouth and took the host
onto his tongue. In that moment, he was flooded by a great peace
and a deep sense that what he had desired, God had desired a

hundred times more. Permit and allow had *nothing* to do with it. Love was the only medium of exchange.

After a time of being with this story, I was struck by how it was a gospel story. I prayed for that man, and for other lepers, and for women and men who feel like lepers in the world and church today, particularly for those who lack the courage to believe how much they are loved yet have the courage to act out of love for the sake of others.

Friday. The final day of my prayer with the leper was a continuation from the previous day. Before my eyes I saw, in place of the gospel scene, settings from our global world: Ethiopians starving . . . undocumented men and women with no place to name as home . . . handicapped children ridiculed by classmates . . . Over and over I offered them into God's hands.

In 1955, Anne Morrow Lindbergh, in *Gift from the Sea*, spoke a message about contemplation and distractions that rings true thirty years later:

> The church is still a great centering force for men and women, more needed than ever before. . . . But . . . our daily life does not prepare us for contemplation. How can a single weekly hour of church, helpful as it may be, counteract the many daily hours of distraction that surround it? If we had our contemplative hour at home we might be readier to give ourselves at church and find ourselves more completely renewed. For the need for renewal is still there. The desire to be accepted whole, the desire to be seen as an individual, not as a collection of functions, the desire to give oneself completely and purposefully pursues us always, and has its part in pushing us into more and more distractions.[2]

With our lives full of distractions, many assumed by the "desire to give oneself completely and purposefully," should we be surprised that our prayer is sometimes full of distractions, making it difficult to savor and to linger in the shadows with God.

Contemplation is a unique form of prayer. Risky because it provides none of the structure guaranteed in rote prayer. Risky because it promises no particular result, like peace, that center-

ing prayer often insures. Risky because its foundation is the conviction that God wants to be near enough to us to reveal to us
what we need to hear to encounter the reality of life on God's
terms and with God's love sustaining us in that reality.

As we prune and pull out weeds to enable fruitful growth,
we may need a reminder that an occasional weed may be a plant
the Lord wishes to water. We may also need a caution not to
pull up what looks like a weed in our neighbor's garden, for to
our neighbor the weed may be a lily.

This chapter closes with a story illustrating this caution.

Children are naturally contemplative. Religions and
churches can encourage this. In Quaker schools, for example, in
most grades children spend up to twenty minutes a day in silent
contemplation. Religions and churches, on the other hand, can
be like other agencies in society that snuff out the contemplative
gifts given to children by God.

Because my husband and I believe that these gifts are to be
encouraged, we have occasionally engaged in a bit of contemplation with our granddaughter since she was fifteen months old.

On the weekend when we celebrated her second birthday,
we took her for a walk across the long meadow that extends from
our daughter's house to the river where we sat on the bank,
stilled for a moment by the beauty of the sun playing through
the leaves and turning the water to gold.

My husband was the first to notice the sounds of the river
that curved beside us and raced over rocks beneath our feet.
"Let's close our eyes and listen to the river. Hear it rush by. Can
you hear how it babbles and sings, Nicole?"

"Grandper! Grandper!"

"Yes, I hear it, too. Rush . . . rush . . . rush goes the brook.
Rushhhh. Rushhhh."

I peek down at my grandaughter. She faces the warmth of
the sun, her eyes tightly closed.

"Grandper!"

"Yes, Nicki. It's lovely, isn't it?"

"GRANDPER!!!"

"What is it, honey?"

"Grandper. *I* hear a chain saw."

Sure enough, far in the distance is the sound of a chain saw.

We celebrated that. We celebrated, with hugs and kisses, that while we heard the river, Nicole heard the chain saw. A few weeks later, to introduce a Day of Recollection, I told this story. A sister across the room spoke up before I had finished. "And she had the courage—she trusted enough to say that she heard something different! Would that we all had the courage and trust of two year olds!"

We who are church community will have that courage and that trust when we who are church institution truly believe that Jesus meant it when he said little ones have a wisdom the learned lack.

11

HARVESTING THE FRUIT

In Old Testament times and in medieval times, bringing in the harvest was worthy of holiday. To reap the fruit of the earth and to gather in celebration evoked a natural mating. In the gospel accounts of the New Testament we find Jesus referring frequently to garden images—sowing the seed, reaping the harvest. Mention of Paul's imagery of ministers' planting and watering and God giving the growth was highlighted in an earlier chapter.

"Whoever remains in me, with me in him, bears fruit in plenty" (Jn 15:56). In the farewell discourse at the Last Supper in John's gospel, Jesus forcefully reminds the disciples that bearing fruit is their call. In fact, he equates bearing fruit and discipleship with the glory of the Father: "It is to the glory of my Father that you should bear much fruit, and then you will be my disciples." And *then* you will be my disciples. How startling this sounds to us who consider discipleship the initial step in the process of ministry. At *harvest* time, Jesus seems to be saying: you, my disciple, will emerge.

For contrasts to the analogies these images present, consider the way we, in the Church today, go about the business of ministry. Although in many church settings evaluation is becoming a process considered constitutive to the ministerial *enterprise,* frequently the focus for evaluation is the *program* or the *project,* and the goal is assessing strengths and weaknesses. The intention here is not to criticize; this style of evaluating the "harvest" is necessary but incomplete.

Times to weigh and measure the fruit of the *ministries* within local and diocesan settings also seem appropriate. Times to celebrate the harvest of a particular ministry or ministries seem as significant as time to prepare *for* ministries. Harvest time for the individual lay minister deserves encouragement and can be initiated by the individual lay minister who takes the time in his or her prayer life to bring to God the fruit-bearing for the glory of God perceived by the lay minister.

Having reflected on readying the soil, planting the seed, watering, weeding, and watching developments, we will now complete our natural progression of spiritual ministerial themes by considering harvesting the fruit, bringing the fruits and future of our ministries to God, contemplatively, in prayer.

Hearkening to the Meaning of Harvest

To delve more deeply into the meaning of harvest, we will return to Vermont and the garden, farmed the French intensive way to bear bountiful fruit.

Winter in Vermont means tobogganing down the hill behind the garden. Spring in Vermont means a stroll down the road to the covered bridge that leads to the back lanes on the other side of the river and a visit to a sugar house where we watch the maple sap boil itself into syrup. Summer in Vermont means tubing down the river as well as watering and weeding.

Fall in Vermont means foliage?

Right. Superb foliage seen through the kitchen windows because fall in Vermont means harvest, and harvest means work—kitchen work.

George and I nearly trip over the harvest on our way into the house. Gone from the back entry are the inner tubes and wading pool and sand pail. In their place are bushel baskets and shopping bags, cornucopias overflowing with winter squash and plum tomatoes, Macintosh apples and pickling cukes, beets and carrots coated with earth that has dried into dust.

But harvest means more than picking the fruit of the earth. Harvest means more than produce to look at. Harvest means tasks to talk about in tones of partisan pride and affection. Leslie tells us that Jeff is trying to make dill pickles for the first time this year. Jeff tells us that Leslie has already put up quarts and quarts of tomato juice. Nicole, standing on a chair at the kitchen table stirring four toy blocks in a pot, tells us, "Make pizza. For supper, Gran. Niki make pizza!"

On Saturday we gaze at the foliage while we core apples and stir tomatoes. Niki helps her grandpa push cooked apples through the Victoria mill screwed to the counter by the sink. I help Leslie lift steaming quarts of apple sauce from the canner. Jeff splits logs. We all tumble into the car at midday to travel to town to buy more jars and a Halloween pumpkin for Niki's Jack o'Lantern.

Sunday morning no one complains of insomnia. Sunday afternoon we are back to "puttin' by for winter" except for Jeff who has gone down to the river with his fishing pole. I label jars, contemplating the harvest colors—crimsom, orange, and dusty rose—of the jars already labeled and lining the window sill where the sun streams in. Leslie and her dad stack the split logs into the small barn while two year old Nicole piles wooden chips onto her plastic sled and pulls it into the barn to put them by for kindling the fires that will keep them warm throughout the winter.

At supper content caresses us all. With her blocks Niki has made more pizza. Jeff has caught five trout. The applesauce is scrumptious. And we've all learned something about the meaning of harvest and the goodness of bearing fruit in plenty in family. On the way back to Boston I began to muse on how what I'd learned about the harvest is applicable to lay ministry.

Savoring the Harvest in Ministry

The harvest is not something to walk away from. It is the culmination of preparation and effort over a long interval. Perhaps Jesus pointed to the importance of fruit-bearing to keep us aware of that. Too often the pace of ministry today, timed to a metronome set by our society, tempts the lay minister to dash forward as soon as one ministerial encounter is over, like a sprinter rushing toward the next encounter that beckons at the top of the next hill. At the risk of sounding radical, may I suggest that it would be better to have *more* lay ministers and *fewer* encounters so that some of the latter can be savored with God?

The harvest is brought into the home—into the heart of the home. Out of sight, out of mind in Vermont would mean fruits and vegetables softening to pulp in the back hall. Out of sight, out of mind in ministry fractures the personal regard intended to be the heart of ministry. "Come home," urges God, "and share with me the faces of the people at the soup kitchen, in the hospital beds, at the parish council meeting. Share with me the children learning to love me, the engaged couples learning to love one another. Share with me the fruit-bearing that the Spirit has accomplished through you."

The harvest is provision for the future. Chopping wood, canning fruits and vegetables, pickling cucumbers take their toll in time and energy, each step eased by collaboration, by the promise that the effort is investment in the future, and by the tactile joy of working with the goods of nature. Taking time to weigh and measure with the Lord, the ministerial encounters we have can feel like struggle, balanced at times by our sensing God's partisan pride and affection that tell us we are true disciples. This affirmation, as well as what is learned by reflecting with the Lord on the fruit-bearing that has come to pass, are our provisions for the future—provisions that feed us so we can go forward and that strengthen us so we can continue to love those whom we are called to shepherd.

The Harvest We Bring to God Turns into God's Harvest

The first year Leslie put up the harvest from the garden she managed with great effort to can a dozen jars of tomatoes. This year the kitchen cupboards can't contain all she has managed to "put by." This year, after Halloween, she called and said that the Jack o'Lantern had become three dozen pumpkin muffins, a pot of pumpkin soup, and a pumpkin and ricotta cheese pie. A chunk of leftover Jack o'Lantern now resides in the freezer waiting for Thanksgiving. In response I kidded her about her learning to imitate the economy of God.

Fall is the time for nature's harvest. Any season can be harvest time in ministry. Initially the lay minister may come to the Lord to contemplate his or her fruit-bearing following *a span of time engaged in ministry.* After some familiarity sensing this dynamic, the lay minister may discover that harvest time in prayer occurs *after every striking ministerial encounter.* When this dynamic develops familiarity, the flow of evaluating fruit-bearing in contemplative prayer may begin to mark the passage of *each ministerial encounter.* Finally, the lay minister may find that *during the actual moment of ministry* a consciousness of God and a sense of savoring the fruit-bearing and/or measuring its quality with the Spirit is happening. In the economy of God, encounter and harvest eventually merge.

How to go about bringing the harvest to contemplative prayer can vary. The New Testament provides some clues. Bragging of course never seemed to earn the praise of Jesus, though the sincere enthusiasm of the returning seventy-two disciples did. Sometimes, on return, the disciples carried a slim harvest in a basket of confusion, but to this Jesus was as open as he was to those times of great fruit-bearing.

Another clue comes from the one who, in the gospel, returned to offer thanksgiving when his companions, who also experienced the Lord's healing, did not. The woman at the well brought to Jesus Samaritans converted by her witness, her personal conviction based on Jesus' perception of the reality of who she was. The fruit-bearing of this woman's ministry of evangelization was that her testimony led Samaritans from the village to a direct encounter and interlude of companionship with Jesus, enabling their heartfelt acclamation of him as "Savior of the world" to emerge from personal, not vicarious, experience.

At harvest time the lay minister's own prayer may mirror some of these dynamics found in the New Testament.

The Proof Is in the Pudding—
God's Harvest Within the Lay Minister

Our view to this point has been from the vantage of the lay minister, e.g., when and how the lay minister measures and weighs his or her fruit-bearing with the Lord in contemplative prayer. Mention was made of sensing affirmation from God, but we would do well to avoid imagery that suggests that God is passively waiting for "results" as if God, through the Spirit, has not been enabling the ministerial fruit-bearing all along. Another unlikely image is that of affirmation that is akin to a pat on the head and a push back to an assembly line characterization of ministry.

God is not an idler. Amid the comings and goings of the minister, *if* the lay minister is struggling with meaningful ministry, *while* the lay minister is struggling with meaningful ministry, *when* the lay minister is engaged in contemplative prayer, God is bearing fruit within this "faithful servant of the Lord."

The signs of this, alluded to earlier in different sections of the text, correspond to the following dynamics:

—"Whose minister am I?" Whether I am St. Mary's or St. Luke's minister, whether I am "helping out Father" or "doing a favor for Sister," are no longer either questions or answers. Within, the lay minister knows with heartfelt conviction, "I am a minister of God."

—The gap between "who I am" and "what I do" is closing because "who I am" and "what I do" are becoming one. God's fruit-bearing is creating integration.

—In ministry and in prayer, making speeches and saying the lines are fading in favor of genuine engagement with the "real," i.e., "doing the scene."

—A more ready recognition of religious experience in ordinary life and a more ready willingness to value the salt of the earth ministry of laity not involved in church ministry are apparent.

—Faith open to change is operative, enabling the lay minister to move beyond acceptance of transformation to a deep desire for ongoing transformation. Spirituality and transformation, as well as ministry and transformation, are perceived as indispensably linked.

No one, least of all me, lays claim to this spiritual development happening overnight. Nor would I ever suggest that any formation program can make the above happen. God, who reaps the harvest, gets the credit for the growing, as Paul said so long ago.

The Bottom Line

This brings us to the bottom line. Mine is a simple but sturdy conviction that the kind of spiritual maturity described above is the fruit-bearing that God is bringing to harvest in a multitude of lay men and women who are fortunate enough to be engaged in meaningful ministry and who are blessed with the desire and the gift to engage in contemplative prayer. This fruit-bearing was initiated by the Holy Spirit in Vatican II and is being activated by the Holy Spirit in the years since the Council.

As I said, that's my bottom line, and I'm not about to budge from it.

There are a number of indications that some parishes and certain dioceses are often unready or unwilling to acknowledge this fruit-bearing that God is bringing about. This is tragic. If resistance to ministerial and spiritual development occurs to "hold back the tide," then spiritual maturity has difficulty finding a foothold. In far too many instances, ministry and spirituality are divorced or encouraged to travel in divergent directions, i.e., spiritually the lay person is considered a pew inhabitant, while ministerially he or she is considered a volunteer, a worker for the church, not God. In far too few instances are professionally trained priests, sisters, brothers, and laity—gifted in spirituality—available to parishes and to lay persons who are engaged in voluntary ministry.

The conscience of the church is challenged by this issue, I believe. Laity who are encouraged to participate in voluntary ministry without the opportunity for spiritual development facilitated by professionally prepared leadership—when possible, lay leadership—are victimized. Teaching lay women and men that baptism and confirmation confer the right to minister yet avoiding the responsibility of enhancing the integration of that ministry with faith in an ongoing and invigorating way runs the risk of encouraging the laity to let themselves be used in an unfree way. In the church, laity hear a great deal about the virtue of serving and very little about manipulation, the sin of using people in a way that disregards respect, call, and their spirituality.

Lay ministers, of course, can victimize a local setting if criteria for their ministry is not established and if evaluation policies and procedures are not in place. But without spiritual and communal support systems offered to laity engaged in voluntary ministry, integrity about criteria and evaluation is a little bit harder to come by, I feel, especially when others in a setting (lay, religious, and clerical) receive compensation that those in voluntary ministry do not. Persons who traditionally have sustained the greater part of ministry in the Church did so under authoritarian structures. The means for evaluating lay ministry (which for the most part has developed since Vatican II) should not be inherited from an earlier period in the church that is "going by the board," in many ways, as a means for evaluating and planning futures for priests, sisters, brothers, and professional lay ministers.

The dynamic of harvest for all men and women engaged in ministry within a setting should, *at the very least,* resonate with the styles and standards of evaluation that many lay people understand and consider *just* within their culture.

Harvesting the Fruit Collaboratively

"We had the experience but missed the meaning." T. S. Eliot's insight could be the motto for parish lay ministers in a multitude of settings. The tradition probably goes back to the disciples on the road to Emmaus. And it was, of course, companionship with Jesus and the light he shed on the revelations of Scripture that led these disciples to discover the *meaning* of what they had experienced.

In this chapter consideration has been given to the individual lay minister contemplating the fruit-bearing of his or her ministry with God in prayer. Encouragement was given to the availability of skilled resource persons with whom the lay minister could confer regarding what's happening in his or her prayer. (Being a realist, I hesitate to say individual spiritual directors because the need so outweighs the availability of professionally prepared directors in most dioceses in the United States.)

Collaborative efforts for reflecting on the harvest often prove fruitful, and are what we will next consider.

Models for Communal, Contemplative Sharing

Gathering together lay ministers for contemplative reflection and prayer can be approached in several different ways. In some instances lay ministers *who participate in the same ministry,* under professional guidance, can experience spiritual enrichment and support in a season of shared prayer with Scripture pertinent to their particular ministries. In other instances, the formation of a group, *cutting across the various ministries* active in a particular local setting, can evoke not only the harmony in diversity to which St. Paul refers, but also an expansion of understanding and praxis through the opportunity of learning from one another.

The first models to be described need facilitation by staff persons with experience and expertise in group dynamics and spirituality. These models can beneficially be employed at the preparatory stage of formation for voluntary ministry or after lay ministers have engaged in ministry for a period of time.

The second set of models depend on an interval of lay experience in ministry for effectiveness as the dynamics center on witness to lay ministry through familiarity with the ministerial encounter.

Planting and Harvesting Models

Ministry in the Gospel Setting. Because the focus of this communal, contemplative model is commonality irregardless of the form of ministry, it is suggested for *mixed groups of ministers.* When I introduced the format with students at Weston, they found that time after time they could identify an experience in their own lives that mirrored the ministerial experience described in the gospel.

Format

Seven participants allows time for each to share during the hour and one half provided every other week for contemplative time together. Because contemplation will be the activity, a ten minute interval for quieting down should be initiated soon after all have come together. The facilitator then introduces the passage from which verses will be used for reflection. An understanding of the evangelist's approach and of the passage, without personal interpretation, provides a necessary framework for the focus but need not extend, ordinarily, beyond ten minutes. The facilitator then introduces the verses for the evening's contemplation, with or without an example from his or her own life, depending on the needs of the group. The participants are invited to share, after an interlude of contemplative silence, an instance remembered when (a) the participant was ministered to in a way similar to that described in the gospel, (b) the participant witnessed another ministering as described in the verses from the passage, or (c) the participant has experienced in his or her own ministry the theme evoked by the selected Scripture.

Following the introduction, the facilitator invites the ministers to contemplate the verses chosen for the evening, e.g., "You received without charge; give without charge. Provide yourselves with no gold or silver, not even with a few coppers for your purses, with no haversack for the journey or spare tunic or footwear or a staff, for the workman deserves his keep" (Mt 10:8b-10).

Remind the participants that this is a contemplative exercise which means being open to whatever images or memories the verses evoke. Hospitality of the heart is a sign of trust in the Lord.

Twenty minutes, designed to the needs of the group, e.g., in silence or with music, in a circle or leaving the room, is appropriate for this segment, with forty minutes allotted to the sharing that follows. The participants are encouraged to continue the dynamic by contemplating one another and the experiences that are shared, letting their own hearts be touched. If, to use the example from the end of the last chapter, one hears "a river" and another hears "a chain saw," both are to find validation in the group. To encourage this, only questions that clarify the experience are invited along with the sharing of feelings experienced by the listeners.

For example, in one session the "no spare tunics" verses elicited from one man a memory of sisters serving in Haiti who subsisted on a material level parallel to those for whom they ministered, going beyond the "bare minimum" only when their own energy to serve would be jeopardized.

A young lay woman in the group found that the verses evoked for her a reflection with the Lord on her life-style of the prior year and a half. In a sixteen month period she had, of necessity, lived in a different place every two months. "Sometimes I wasn't sure where I would lay down my head at night." She closed her sharing by revealing that reflecting on that particular directive to the earliest disciples had deepened the meaning of her own life and the importance of its style as a preparation for ministry.

After a quiet moment, an elderly sister began to speak, and as she did, tears moved down her lined face. "In the forty years I have been a nun, I have always been in a situation where one dime would put me in touch by phone with the motherhouse or convent where some other nun would answer the phone and dispatch some other nun to pick me up. I thought what I lived was the vow of poverty." Sister touched the young lay woman's hand. "Thank you for sharing with me what it really means when it *is* lived."

Often the sharing segment of the gathering leads spontaneously into prayer as it did in this instance when we together called out for the courage to leave behind not only spare tunics but also any rigidity about what that means in our own lives and the lives of others.

Perceiving experientially a likeness between ministry today and ministry in gospel times is of inestimable value in helping lay ministers form, interiorly, a ministerial identity or in reinvigorating an identity already in the making. In addition, this activity, and the one that follows, further an understanding of spirituality as intimacy with God through my way of being with others in the world.

Spirituality in Life Settings

Our second model highlights the *lay* dimension inherent in lay ministry, for it encourages those engaged in ministry to *notice manifestations of God in their everyday lives.* It works best when there is a professional guide for every eight to twelve participants. The make-up of the group that gathers weekly can be laity from several ministries within the parish together with priests, religious and laity on staff. In a ten week program the sessions in the *first half* should focus on helping the participants to notice (especially their feelings), to articulate some things about themselves to one another, and to listen to each other in a contemplative way. This segment furthers ministerial sensitivities. Input from leaders must be minimal in order to encourage the participants to focus on one another. It is essential that the leaders of the program emphasize to participants the value of and need for *confidentiality.*

During the *second half* of the program, each participant is invited to share an instance from the past week that he or she would identify as a religious experience. In the beginning some participants may feel a need to listen without sharing, and the facilitator is wise to encourage this freedom. Questions that help clarification without making value judgments on the experience are encouraged.

For example, one young lay minister described being alone with his grandmother when the grandmother suddenly collapsed. The young man, at first, felt a rush of anxiety as he frantically, and unsuccessfully, tried to contact other members of the family. Riding in an ambulance to the hospital emergency room with his grandmother, the young man began to experience a sense of "being carried." As he waited in the emergency room, remembering many poignant times shared with his grandmother, the young man had a strong sense of God's presence that deepened when he was allowed to remain with his grandmother in a hospital room.

"What was wrong with your grandmother?" As the facilitator notes that questions are centering on the physical details of the situation, he or she asks the lay minister if he can "tell us a little more about when his heart moved from anxiety to hope."

As participants begin to "own" their life experience, several developments may emerge:

—a more caring and sensitive noticing of the fabric of daily life.

—a sense that God is encountered and can be savored in settings other than prayer and liturgy.

—increased freedom to trust other ministers and to share with them the stories of God narrated by their lives.

—increased responsibility about listening to others and about accepting the stories of God that colleagues tell.

For lay ministers one value of this means of harvesting the fruit that faith enables is an affirmation of the *lay* dimensions of their lives—family, work in secular settings, civic and social involvements. The lay ministers may come to perceive that the "ordinary" and secular orientation of their lives is a gift brought to ministry rather than a handicap that has to be hidden or overcome *in order* to minister effectively.

Within the articulation experience of those who minister within the parish, trust is engendered; within the listening experience of those who minister within the parish, empathy is engendered. In one instance, for example, several lay ministers expressed a greater appreciation for the challenges an associate pastor faced when he shared his discouragement in preparing a homily for a liturgy celebrating his brother and sister-in-law's twenty-fifth anniversary.

Five times during the week I sat at my desk with the scriptural passage and nothing happened. Nothing! Blank! Zero! A half hour before the liturgy, walking over to their parish church, I felt a terrible panic. What would I say? Five minutes before the Mass started I walked over to the lectern and looked at the passage again, and there it was. There it was, beside the gospel passage, just what I was to say. It flashed through my mind as if God was writing what I couldn't find words to express. For someone who's always chastizing his brother priests for inadequately preparing their homilies, it was startling to discover that there are times, even in the most familiar task, when one can fall short and get yanked by the collar to rely on God.

Men and women who share their own sense of God in their lives no longer perceive one another as rivals. These ministers move from looking at one another to liking one another to loving one another to living with one another in that harmony frequently characterized as holy.

Like to Like Spiritual/Ministerial Sharing

In this model, lay ministers *sharing the same ministry* gather to pray, either consecutively over an interval of time or on days of recollection or retreats. The leader's role is to enhance the mutuality inherent in the ministry. Mutuality, in this instance, does not mean sameness; rather it implies the enrichment sensed by the diversity evoked when different aspects of the same experience are savored.

Following are models for gatherings *for shared reflection,* one for lectors and another for eucharistic ministers. Patterns for each session are similar to those described for the prior group activities.

Lectors

First Session—Seeing Scripture as Story
. . . the story of a people as well as the story of God. Half the group contemplates what that meant in Old and New Testament times; half the group contemplates what that means today. Sharing in small groups first, then in large group.

Second Session—Contemplating the Church and Scripture
. . . Possible topics for contemplation and sharing:
The Church as Hearer of the Word
The Church as Proclaimer of Good News

The Word within the Liturgical Season
The Word within the Liturgy

Third Session—Contemplating the Lector as Hearer of the Word
. . . Topic for contemplation and sharing: "Listen, anyone who has ears to hear!" (As lector I am one of the first to hear Sunday's word, what that means to me. Or comparing my experience of hearing the Word while seated with the congregation and my experience of hearing the word when I lector.)

Fourth Session—Contemplating Those Who Originally Heard the Word
. . . Possible hearers for contemplation and sharing: Abraham, Jacob, Hannah, Mary and Martha, Peter, Paul

Fifth Session—Contemplating Themes within God's Word
. . . Possible themes for contemplation and sharing: God's Presence: 1 Kings 19:9-14; Love: 1 Cor 13:1-13, 1 John 4:7-8

Sixth Session—Contemplating the Word and Parish Community
. . . Possible themes for contemplation and sharing: Savoring your community that has listened to the word; lingering in the shadows of its deafness to the word. Praying for those with whom you minister (other lectors, other lay men and women engaged in voluntary ministry, parish team: 1 Cor 3:5-9).

Seventh Session—Contemplating Stories of Faith
Reflect on and share the stories of faith told by those whom the lectors meet in their neighborhoods, at work—remember these with the Lord.

Eucharistic Ministers

Using a similar dynamic, the eucharistic ministers reflect, share and pray with the following themes:
Super-abundance of Providential Love: The dragnet (Lk 5:1-

11); parable of the Father's love (Lk 15:3-24); loaves and fishes (Mt 14:13-21; 15:21-39)

The Generosity of Jesus: The Good Samaritan (Lk 10:29-37); I am the vine, you are the branches (Jn 15:5-10); the feast in the kingdom (Lk 14:15-24)

Remembering those who have shared the sacrament with you, letting their presence emerge again and, from the heart, asking the Lord's blessing on them.

Remembering those who may desire to share the table of the Lord but who do not at this time because of struggles or distance related to faith.

Remembering those who, like eucharistic ministers, participate in nourishing others (parents and infants; those who care for the elderly and those who care for men and women who are mentally or physically ill; those with a sensitivity of spirit who evoke hope where there is despair, faith where there is doubt).

By savoring and lingering in the shadows *together,* ministers bear the fruit of community.

Celebrating Our Colleagues in Ministry

Our last model, borrowed from a parish I visited in another diocese, exemplifies affirming in a festive way the contributions to the parish community made by lay men and women engaged in a particular voluntary ministry. Although the hosts for the evening's celebration are colleagues involved in other voluntary ministries, the celebration is open to the whole parish and provides an introduction to ministry for other parishioners.

A local community may want to signify harvest time during the autumn season by a celebration each year dedicated to a different ministry exercised in the parish. Because the design of the celebration should be the creation of the lay ministers within the local setting, drawing on the talents unique to the community, the description of an evening I experienced is offered more to whet appetites than to provide a blueprint.

The ushers at St. Rita's thought it strange that Saturday night was chosen as the meeting night to launch their new year of ministry. The Sunday before, several said as much to one another; not one of them looked forward to lengthy discussions about planning the coffee hour after the ten o'clock Sunday Mass and introductory sessions for new ushers.

What the ushers did not know was that lectors and ministers of music were, behind the scenes, working on the appreciation celebration for those who faithfully, fair weather or foul, exercised the ministry of hospitality. Nor could they understand, soon after gathering in the rectory, why Fr. Burns wanted them to move along to the parish hall to reassess the facility for coffee hours. That had never before seemed necessary.

Who among them could have guessed that ten minutes later they would be seated center front listening to the ministers of music welcoming *them* with what the M.C., Pat Daniello, called the theme song each usher seemed to hum to the stranger as well as the friend at St. Rita's: "Consider Yourself One of Us" from "Oliver."

But that was only the beginning.

In a twinkling the stage was emptied, the lights in the parish hall dimmed, and Mae McFarland, the oldest lector and one of the best, was sitting on stage, a spotlight on her as she reminisced about hospitality in her home and in the parish while she was growing up. "Many the afternoon I'd come home from school to find my mother reading tea leaves around the kitchen table with one or another of the neighbor women. They just did it for fun but it was a rare day my mother wasn't offering hospitality to someone on the block. It might be dangerous today but my pa always taught us kids that if you meet a stranger on the street before seven in the morning you always say hello to him." Mae paused then to offer a bit of her own hospitality, calling out, "'Lo, Charley. C'mon down front. Better late than never. C'mon now, we're glad you're here!'

"For some reason or other, we lived in a French neighborhood but went to the Irish Church. Oh, I remember why we went to the Irish church—because my pa was Irish!"

Charley, now seated in the front, gave a hoot. "That's as good a reason as any, Mae."

"Well, one of the ushers, Mr. Kelly, you remember him, Charley? He lived in our neighborhood. Everytime I met him on the street he'd say, 'Hi, Mae. How are you today?' It felt real good to have him speak to me because, with everyone else in the neighborhood going to the French church, I didn't know any grown-ups except the people on either side of us. Sometimes Mr. Kelly would say, 'You want a ride to church next Sunday, Mae, you just give Mr. Kelly a call.' I always wanted to do that but Pa said the Lord gave me two good legs so I had no reason to do it." Mae laughed then paused to wipe her eyes. "A good man and a good usher, Mr. Kelly. May he rest in peace." After a silent moment, she sighed. "We live in a different age today," Mae said in closing.

Pat joined her on stage to introduce slides that illustrated for the community the loss of hospitality and the depersonalization that, with increased frequency, characterizes our age and makes even more necessary and meaningful the ministry of the ushers at St. Rita's.

After the slides Stella Wascyk, accompanied on the piano by her husband Peter, sang "Sing Along" songs celebrating hospitality, starting with "Won't You Come with Me Lucille (in My Merry Oldsmobile)?"

The next segment of the program featured skits written and produced by the lectors, ribbing the ushers for inappropriate "greeting gregariousness" of which no usher at St. Rita's was guilty. *Mike the Manager* received a boo or two, but cheers for *Thomas of a Thousand Welcomes* raised the roof.

When the crowd had quieted down, the MC invited a representative from each of the other ministries operative in the parish to the stage where a religious educator, a hospital visitor, a social justice advocate, a eucharistic minister, and an evangelizer each witnessed to how hospitality was a crucial factor in the designated ministry in which he or she was involved. The

ushers were then invited to the stage and given a small memento
by one of the other lay ministers. Party refreshments were served
after the finale—a rousing rendition of "Show Me, Don't Tell
Me" from "My Fair Lady."

Sharing the Bounty

Now and again a concern is raised about the possibility that
the expansion of lay ministries within the Church will draw lay
people away from mission to the world by encouraging them to
fixate on internal church matters. Dolores Leckey, Executive
Director of the NCCB Secretariat of the Laity, though more
aware of this dilemma than most, is hopeful: "Respected
authentic participation in the life and conduct of the Church's
internal agenda improves the Church's ability to minister to the
world."

One reason for this optimism may be that participation in
church by many through ministerial activity can create local
communities more vibrant in faith. People energized with faith,
caring about their civic and global responsibilities, contribute to
renewing, with peace and justice efforts, our land and world.

For this to happen, however, I feel that we must be *inten-
tional* about it happening. The initiation of lay ministry on the
parish level is little more than ten years old in most places. First
efforts were, quite naturally, directed toward teaching the "how
to" of each particular ministry. Because the *activity* of each voluntary ministry is limited in scope, the ministry provides a good
setting for a formation process that includes spiritual development *and apostolic development* linked to mission in the world.
Feasibility, of course, is not rationale. Because the ultimate purpose of ministry is to serve God by enhancing mission to the
broader world, apostolic development should be as constitutive
to formation for voluntary ministry as spiritual development is.
The enemy of this process is any perception that fosters a
"church worker" mentality about lay ministry on the local level.
As mentioned earlier, now is the hour of temptation for con-
structing a vast new civil service type bureaucracy built on the
backs of volunteers. On the other hand, now is the hour when
parish staff can help God create a multitude of ministers,

enriched by spiritual and apostolic formation. Confronting this either/or is the task of every local community and diocese.

This chapter will close with descriptions of two models that encourage apostolic formation as part of the development of ministries in the local community.

Christian Service Model

On Saturday, December 15, 1984, Gerry and Patti McKenna-Lee were commissioned as Maryknoll Lay Missioners at Maryknoll, New York. After six months of language study in Bolivia, Gerry, Patti, and their two children will serve the poor of Venezuela. Gerry, after graduation from Weston, was a lay minister on the staff of an affluent North Shore parish in the Boston archdiocese. As part of his pastoral responsibilities, Gerry facilitated Christian Service, a program that encouraged parishioners to engage in some form of charitable outreach or social action within broader communities. Hundreds of parishioners, regardless of their particular ministerial involvement *within* the parish, pledged to participate in one endeavor *beyond* the parish. The offerings ranged from a commitment to donate blood to the Red Cross once during the year, to working regularly at Rosie's Place (a facility for poor and homeless women in inner-city Boston), to participating on a Central American Action Committee. One responsibility of the Social Justice Committee, which was part of the Christian Service Program, was to educate and expand the horizons of those serving in these various endeavors. The process provided by this suburban parish evoked significant integrative factors related to ministry, parish, and mission.

Because it affirms the freedom of the lay person to choose among diverse involvements, the Christian Service model is particularly appropriate for a parish where a variety of perspectives regarding charitable outreach and social justice exist. Within this structure, the witness of parish participants is an important educative element. The investment of a professional staff member's time and energy in the facilitation of the Christian Service component of parish life reveals the priority placed on lay mission to the world by this parish community. Gerry and Patti's decision, after six years of dedication to the parish, to further their own apostolic thrust for the sake of our brothers and sisters in Latin America makes a powerful statement, emerging from the midst of parish life, about commitment to God and commitment to neighbors truly in need.

Ministerial Partnerships for Mission

Bonding between pairs of voluntary ministries on the local level provides another model for making mission constitutive to ministry in a parish. Harmony is evoked when diverse ministries unite for a common purpose beyond a given locale. To link together ministries with compatible components is easier than one might suppose. The following grouping is but one instance of such a bonding:

Ministries	*Mission*
Religious Educators and Lectors	Education for Proclaiming the Good News of Peace and Justice
Social Advocates and Eucharistic Ministers	Famine Relief and U.S. Food Programs
Hospitality and Marriage Ministers	The Homeless and Domestic Violence

Participatory Dynamics for Bearing Fruit

As the numbers and kinds of lay voluntary ministers and ministries increase within parishes and dioceses, boards composed of representatives from the various voluntary ministries can be established to help in the coordination of the ministries. Membership on the boards would also be open to professional coordinators of lay ministries.

Ways to harmonize and integrate the ministries, evaluation of developmental needs regarding ministries and ministers, planning spiritual and mission components that are intra-parish and inter-diocese—these are examples of the kinds of activities in which a board might be engaged. The advent of a board in a given locale can insure that the stories told about voluntary ministry are not horror stories.

Good stories provide the best guarantee that the good news will be heard! Good dynamics—ones that are just and enabling—provide the structural support that eventually bear the fruit of good stories proclaiming the good news!

POSTSCRIPT—
MULCHING FOR THE FUTURE

"Hoppy Birfday to you,
"Hoppy Birfday to you,
"Hoppy Birfday, dear Dad,
"Hoppy Birfday to you."

Silence.

"Hoppy Birfday, Dad. Dad, don't you want a hoppy birf-day? I'm giving you a hoppy birfday present."

Silence.

"Daaaaad! Don't you want a hoppy birfday?"

At 6:30 A.M., four months before his natal date, on Thanksgiving morning, after a late, late night with Trivial Pursuit (having been beaten by Katherine and Tierney), Nicole's dad, Jeff, is sipping coffee with one eye open and on Niki for safety's sake. Finally he manages a slow show of gratitude. "Thank you, Niki. Happy Birthday and Happy Thanksgiving to you."

In bed and barely awake myself, I feel a sense of wonder and gratitude at how much our little one has come to learn in the two years of her young life. I am alert enough to notice that she is integrating into her contemplative knowing memory and imagination, remembering images from her own birthday a month earlier, imagining her father's birthday.

Children, naturally contemplative, are the best teachers of the process. They approach life, the reality before them, contemplatively: with openness, noticing, letting themselves be drawn by what they notice, staying with it and the feelings that emerge, expressing those feelings. What absorbs their attention eventually reveals something to them, and through the process of discovery they learn. They learn that round pegs fit in round holes, that wheels turn, that water is wet. No one has to tell them; if someone tries to tell them, they often don't understand so do not learn. Contemplating ... exploring ... discovering ... learning.

They learn that momma's arms around them feel good. They learn that their arms around a teddy bear feel good. Contemplation leads to revelation. Contemplation and revelation teach the child to be relational.

Then he or she troops off to elementary school where the mind and reason are encouraged. Hour upon hour facts are "mastered" and information is gathered (perhaps assisted by a computer)—none of it necessarily deepening the relational sensibilities within the child.

For the relational to be evoked, contemplation is essential.

That is a *fact;* that is a fact of *global* import.

On Thanksgiving Day Nicole yawned when Pam tried to explain that she was *engaged,* would be getting *married,* would invite Niki to the *wedding.* But at dinner Niki's eyes lit up and her mouth broke into a big smile. Looking at me, she cried, "You're Grandper's Gran!"

She had discovered our relationship contemplatively; meaning had erupted and with it excitement.

I pointed to Leslie and asked her who Leslie was.

"That's my mudder."

I pointed to Jeff.

"That's my mudder."

We all laughed and started kidding one another. Niki would have none of it. She leaned forward, past Tierney who was between her and Jeff, and said in a consoling yet earnest voice: "You *are* my mudder, *too,* Dad!"

Mother had meaning for her and, relationally, Jeff is included in that meaning. She wants it that way. The meaning has nothing to do with gender or role. It has to do *with love, with being relational.*

At times contemplation in our culture is mentioned nostalgically as if the commentator is mystified, not only because it is no longer with us, but also by the occasional yearning for it that puts in an appearance now and then. I sensed that in Enid Nemy's *New Yorkers etc.* column entitled "What To Do When

There's Not Much to Do But Wait." In an informal poll connected to the subject, Ms. Nemy found that some folks prepare for that eventuality by bringing work along, putting to good use every available moment and not wasting time contemplating the life around them.[1]

Ernest Hebert in a *Boston Globe* column mourns the loss of contemplation and probes the cause: "The demise of the front porch symbolizes the decline of what the porch was best for: contemplation."

Life was different when houses featured front porches. "New homes aren't even built with front porches. Meanwhile the subtle art of contemplation is going to be eclipsed in our world."

Hebert notes the seriousness of this eclipse:

> These days we have meditation. . . . We have alcohol and drugs and television to help put the mind on cruise, often at great price to health. But we do not have contemplation. Meditation relaxes the mind by emptying it; contemplation relaxes the mind by pruning and arranging the familiar things of our surroundings.[2]

In that pruning and arranging we discover meaning in the only way that meaning can be found. A world or culture or church where contemplation is on the decline is hastening toward becoming a world or culture or church *without* meaning.

By sharing with you the means and the value of combining ministry with contemplative approaches to life and prayer, my hope is that you will feel encouraged to discover meaning beyond ministry by discovering meaning within ministry. Or, to put it another way: May the mission, to which we as church are called, start with contemplation and end with fruit-bearing because we have discovered how to savor and linger in the shadows within the ministries to which we have been newly called by the Source of all meaning, ministry and mission.

Blessings—as you practice the art of contemplation in your own faith and ministry!

NOTES

2. Claiming What Is Owned

1. Karl Rahner, S.J., "The Experience of God Today," in *Theological Investigations,* Vol. 11, Seabury Press, 1974.

3. "Does It Make a Difference?"

1. William Barry, S.J. and William Connelly, S.J., *The Practice of Spiritual Direction,* Seabury Press, 1982, p. 47.
2. John Shea, *Praying* #1, NCR, p. 36.

4. In the Old Testament Yahweh Ministers

1. John Dominic Crossan, "Judges," *The Jerome Biblical Commentary,* Prentice-Hall, p. 152.
2. R.A.F. MacKenzie, S.J., "Job," *The Jerome Biblical Commentary,* p. 512.
3. *Ibid.,* p. 513.
4. James Dickey, *God's Images,* Oxmoor House, 1977.
5. Demetrius R. Dumm, O.S.B., "Tobit, Judith, Esther," *The Jerome Biblical Commentary,* p. 631.
6. *Ibid.,* p. 632.
7. Bruce Vawter, C.M., "Introduction to Prophetic Literature," *The Jerome Biblical Commentary.*
8. *Ibid.*
9. *Ibid.*
10. T.W. Manson, *The Servant Messiah,* Cambridge University Press, 1961.
11. Oscar Cullman, *The Christology of the New Testament,* SCM Press, 1959, pp. 52–82.
12. *Ibid.*
13. *Ibid.*
14. Roland E. Murphy, "Introduction to Wisdom Literature," *The Jerome Biblical Commentary,* pp. 487–494.

5. In the New Testament Jesus Ministers

1. Cullman, *op. cit.*
2. Manson, *op. cit.*
3. *Ibid.*
4. *Ibid.*
5. *Ibid.*

6. In the Faithful the Holy Spirit Ministers

1. St. Basil the Great, *On the Holy Spirit,* St. Vladimir's Seminary Press, 1980, pp. 76–78.
2. *Ibid.,* p. 16.
3. Yves Congar, *I Believe in the Holy Spirit,* Seabury Press, 1983.
4. Jurgen Moltmann, *The Church in the Power of the Spirit,* Harper & Row, 1977, p. 306.
5. *Ibid.*
6. *Ibid.*
7. Congar, *op. cit.*
8. Karl Adam as quoted in *With Bright Wings—A Book of the Spirit,* ed. Mary Grace Swift, Paulist Press, 1976, pp. 36–37.
9. John Shea, *An Experience Named Spirit,* Thomas More, 1983, p. 217.
10. Adam, *op. cit.,* Swift, pp. 186–187.
11. Shea, *op. cit.*
12. Delp, in Swift, *op. cit.,* p. 215.
13. Barth, in Swift, *op. cit.,* p. 197.
14. Delp, in Swift, *op. cit.*
15. Louis Dupre, *The Other Dimension,* Doubleday, 1972, p. 475.
16. Ignatius of Loyola, *The Spiritual Exercises.*
17. Barat, in Swift, op. cit.
18. Lawrence Cunningham, *The Catholic Heritage,* Crossroad, 1983.
19. Lawrence Cunningham, *The Meaning of Saints,* Harper & Row, 1980, pp. 154–155. Emphasis added.
20. *Ibid.*
21. *Ibid.*

22. *Ibid.*

23. Marcy Heidish, *Miracles,* New American Library, 1984, p. 305.

24. Moltmann, *op. cit.,* p. 34.

24. Congar, *op. cit.*

25. McMahon, in Swift, *op cit.,* p. 206.

26. Swift, *op. cit.*

27. Congar, *op. cit.*

28. Ann Bedford Ulanov, *Receiving Woman: Studies in the Psychology and Theology of the Feminine,* p. 103.

29. Moltmann, *op. cit.,* p. 62.

30. Thomas Morton, "Hagia Sophia," *The Collected Poems of Thomas Morton,* New Directions, 1977, p. 369.

31. Von le Fort, *Hymns to the Church,* "Pentecost," in Swift, *op. cit.*

7. Discerning Basic Elements of Ministry

1. National Conference of Catholic Bishops, *Called and Gifted,* United States Catholic Conference, 1980.

2. *Ibid.*

3. *Ibid.*

10. Watering, Weeding, Watching Developments

1. David Fleming, S.J., *A Contemporary Reading of the Spiritual Exercises,* The Institute of Jesuit Sources, 1976.

2. Anne Morrow Lindbergh, *Gift from the Sea,* Random House, 1955, pp. 54–55.

Postscript

1. Enid Nemy, "What to Do When There's Not Much to Do But Wait," in *New Yorkers Etc., The New York Times,* August 11, 1982.

2. Ernest Hebert, "Rooms With a View," *Boston Sunday Globe,* June 12, 1983.

BIBLIOGRAPHY

Ministry and Mission

CALLED AND GIFTED: THE AMERICAN CATHOLIC LAITY—
Statement of the bishops of the United States affirming the place
of laity within the Church.
USCC Publishing Services, Washington, D.C.

OFFICIAL MINISTRY IN A NEW AGE—Editor, James Provost
Permanent Seminar Studies #3
Canon Law Society, Catholic University, 1981

THE CATHOLIC HERITAGE—Lawrence Cunningham
*(Martyrs, Ascetics, Pilgrims, Warriors, Mystics, Theologians, Art-
ists, Humanists, Activists, Outsiders, Saints)*
Crossroad, 1983

THE LAY-CENTERED CHURCH—Leonard Doohan
Winston Press, Minneapolis, 1984

THE MEANING OF SAINTS—Lawrence Cunningham
Harper & Row, 1980

GIFTS THAT DIFFER—David Power
Pueblo, NY, 1981

FULL CHURCH, EMPTY RECTORY-*Training Lay Ministers for
Parishes Without Priests*
Dennis Geaney
Fides Claretian, Notre Dame, IN, 1980

CHALLENGE TO THE LAITY—Editor, Russell Barta
Our Sunday Visitor, Huntington, IN, 1980
Laity in Mission Within the World

GROWING TOGETHER—NCCB CONFERENCE ON SHARED
MINISTRY
Nouwen, Weakland, Finn, Cummins, Greer, Monroe, Ponce
U.S. Catholic Conference, Washington, D.C.

THE MAKING OF A PASTORAL PERSON—Rev. Gerald R. Niklas
Alba House, Staten Island, NY, 1980

GIFTS—*A Laity Reader*
Selected Articles from the Gifts Journal, 1979–1983

NCCB Bishops' Committee on the Laity Office
U.S. Catholic Conference, Washington, D.C.
CONVERTS, DROPOUTS, RETURNEE—*A Study of Religious Change Among Catholics*
Dean Hoge,
U.S. Catholic Conference, Washington, D.C.

History

THE RENEWAL OF AMERICAN CATHOLICISM—David J. O'Brien
Paulist Press, NY, 1972
POPULAR RELIGION IN THE MIDDLE AGES—Rosalind and Christopher Brooke
Thames and Hudson, London, 1984
NATURE, MAN & SOCIETY IN THE TWELFTH CENTURY— Marie D. Chenu
University of Chicago Press, 1957
TRADITIONS, TENSIONS, TRANSITION IN MINISTRY— Twenty-Third Publications, Mystic, CT, 1982
THE CHURCH AND LAITY FROM NEWMAN TO VATICAN II— Jean Guitton
Alba House, Staten Island, NY, 1965
AMERICAN CATHOLICS—James Hennessey
Oxford University Press, NY, 1981
PEOPLE IN THE CHURCH—Yves Congar
Newman Press, NY, 1965

Parish

MODELS OF CHURCH—Avery Dulles
Doubleday, Garden City, NY, 1977
THE CHRISTIAN PARISH—William J. Bausch
Fides Claretian, Notre Dame, IN, 1980
THE PARISH: A PEOPLE, A MISSION, A STRUCTURE—A vision statement of the Bishops' Committee on the Parish.
USCC Publishing Services, Washington, D.C.
WHO ARE WE AND WHERE ARE WE GOING?—William C. Harms
William H. Sadlier, Inc., New York, NY

THE PARISH SELF-STUDY GUIDE—A workbook based upon the bishops' vision statement *The Parish: A People, A Mission, A Structure* that helps a parish evaluate its strengths and weaknesses. USCC Publishing Services, Washington, D.C.

THE PRACTICAL GUIDE FOR PARISH COUNCILS—William J. Rademacher
Twenty-Third Publications, Mystic, CT

TODAY'S PARISH—A monthly magazine
Twenty-Third Publications, Mystic, CT

BUILDING THE LOCAL CHURCH *Shared Responsibility in Diocesan Pastoral Councils*—NCCB Bishops' Committee on the Laity
USCC Catholic Conference

Spirituality

SEASONS OF STRENGTH—New Visions of Adult Christian Maturing (1984)

CHRISTIAN LIFE PATTERNS: *The Psychological Challenges and Religious Invitation to Adult Life.*
Evelyn Whitehead and James Whitehead
Doubleday, Garden City, NY

THE PRACTICE OF SPIRITUAL DIRECTION
William A. Barry & William J. Connolly
The Seabury Press, NY, 1982

THE ORDINARY WAY—*A Family Spirituality*
Dolores R. Leckey
Crossroad, NY, 1982

CHRISTIANS AT PRAYER—Editor, John Gallen, S.J.
University of Notre Dame, Liturgical Studies, 1977

NOISY CONTEMPLATION—William Callahan
Quixote Center, Mt. Rainier, MD

STORIES OF GOD—John Shea

STORIES OF FAITH—John Shea

EXPERIENCE OF THE SPIRIT—John Shea
Thomas More Press

STAGES OF FAITH: THE PSYCHOLOGY OF HUMAN DEVELOPMENT AND THE QUEST FOR MEANING
James Fowler
Harper & Row, NY, 1981

THE SPIRITUALITY OF FRIEDRICH VON HUGEL—Joseph Whalen, S.J.
Newman Press, 1971

CELTIC INCANTATIONS—Alexander Carmichael
   Vineyard, 1978
MAY I HATE GOD?—Pierre Wolff
   Paulist Press, NY, 1979
THE TREE OF HOPE—*National Conference on Lay Spirituality in America*
   Bishops' Committee on the Laity
   U.S. Catholic Conference, Washington, D.C.
WOMEN OF SPIRIT—*Female Leadership in Jewish and Christian Traditions*
   Editors, Rosemary Ruether and Eleanor McLaughlin
   Simon & Schuster, NY, 1979
MIRYAM OF NAZARETH—*Woman of Strength & Wisdom*
   Ann Johnson
   Ave Maria Press, Notre Dame, IN, 1984
A-WAY IN THE WORLD: *Family Life as Spiritual Discipline*
   Ernest Boyer
   Harper & Row, NY, 1984
THE DAYS AND THE NIGHTS—*Prayers for Today's Woman*
   Editor, Candida Lund
   Image Books Doubleday Garden City, NY, 1980
WHAT IMAGE AM I AS A WOMAN OF PRAYER?
   Dot Hortsmann and Mary Sullivan R.C.
   At Home Retreats 1984
GIFTS—Newsletter for Laity
   NCCB Bishops' Committee on the Laity
   Washington, D.C.

Associations and Additional Resources

National Pastoral Musicians Association
225 Sheridan Street, NW
Washington DC 20011

National Catholic Education Association
Washington, D.C.

National Association of Church Personnel Administrators
100 East Eighth St., Cincinnati, OH 45202

Publications: LAY PERSONNEL POLICIES Sr. Barbara Garland

National Pastoral Life Center
299 Elizabeth Street, New York, NY, 10012
CHURCH—magazine (quarterly) on pastoral life in the Church.
Clearinghouse for information on pastoral ministry, consultant service.

ORIGINS—Selections from current documents and presentations on Church, weekly.
National Catholic News Service, 1312 Massachusetts Avenue, NW, Washington, D.C. 20005.

Alliance of Catholic Laity
110 So. Dearborn Street, Room 820
Chicago, IL 60603

National Center for the Laity
Newsletter—"Initiatives"
Laity in World
14 E. Chestnut Street, Chicago, IL 60611

Association for the Rights of Catholics in the Church
PO Box 3932, Philadelphia, PA 19146

National Association for Lay Ministry
(Members are men and women engaged in both professional and voluntary ministry.) Newsletter, national convention.
12461 West Dakota Drive, Lakewood, CO 80228

The Center for the Ministry of the Laity (Laity in World)
Andover Newton Theological School
210 Herrick Road, Newton Center, MA

St. Vincent Pallotti Center for Apostolic Development
797 Monroe Ave NE, Washington, DC

Volunteers for Educational and Social Services
Texas Catholic Conference, 3002 So. Congress Avenue, Austin, TX

International Liaison
U.S. Catholic Coordinating Ctr. for Lay Volunteer Ministries, Suite
    100
1234 Mass. Avenue, NW, Washington, DC

United States Catholic Conference
1312 Massachusetts Avenue, NW
Washington, D.C. 20005